meredisciple

a spiritual guide
for emerging leaders

JEFF STRONG

ISBN: 978-0-557-41973-9

*I cry because the future has once again found its sparkle
and has grown a million times larger.
And I cry because I am ashamed of how badly I have treated
the people I love–of how badly I behaved
during my own personal Dark Ages–back before
I had a future and someone who cared for me from above.
It is like today the sky opened up and only now am I allowed to enter.*

~ Douglas Coupland

For Lauren Emily Strong and Kara Aveline Strong

God has given me a song.
Without your mother I would not have found the courage to sing.
Without you I would not have found the lyrics.

table of contents

Acknowledgements i

Introduction iv

Part I: Foundations

1. In His Dust 1
2. The Transforming Vision 14
3. Wild Beasts and Angels 35

Part II: Money, Sex, and Power

4. A Good Eye 57
5. The Beautiful Risk 73
6. A Voice in the Wilderness. 100

Part III: Into the Kingdom

7. The Four Loves 119
8. Tikkun Olam 135
9. A Tree of Life 147

acknowledgements

It's been a dream of mine to one day write a book, especially one focused on helping emerging leaders follow Jesus more faithfully. I struggled as a teenager with my faith, and while the local church I was connected to offered tremendous support, care, and empowerment, it wasn't until I attended Redeemer University College that my faith began to flourish. At Redeemer I was pushed to think through the whole-life implications of my decision to follow Jesus, and was surrounded by people who were passionate about understanding what discipleship to Jesus meant for their everyday lives.

I'm incredibly thankful for the education I received at Redeemer, but I'm acutely aware that most of the young adults I come into contact with will choose not to attend a Christian University like Redeemer. While I recognize that Christian university education isn't for everyone, I believe that learning to think deeply and broadly about the nature and implications of discipleship is. That's why I wrote *Mere Disciple*; to provide emerging leaders with an introductory framework from which to build an authentic and transformative relationship with Jesus.

Although this book cites me as the author, very few of these ideas are my own. *Mere Disciple* is a collection of wisdom from many sources, not the least of which are special people God has placed in my life over the past fifteen years. Whatever insights contained within this book are true, noble, admirable, and praiseworthy (Philippians 4:8), I'm indebted to the people and relationships that gave rise to them.

Specifically, I would like to thank the following people for their contributions to this book:

Thanks to Anne Plessl for doing her best to ensure my words and ideas retain coherence and clarity. You were a pleasure to work with and I'm so glad you offered your assistance. This book is immeasurably better for it.

Thanks to David Adams for giving me the space to stretch myself and my gifts. Very few emerging leaders have been given the chance to work with someone as gracious, empowering, and fun. Thanks for giving me a shot.

Thanks to Andy Montgomery for his enormous contributions to this entire project. From interior design, cover design, and web design I can honestly say this book wouldn't have made it to press without you! Thank you so much for your servant heart and consistent encouragement. I look forward to future projects with you as an integral part of the creative process.

Thanks to Al Wolters of Redeemer University College for generously offering to help sharpen my thinking on Christian worldview, history, and dualism. Our times together were deeply formative for me personally and theologically.

Thanks to Matt Pamplin and Cynthia Van Dalen of Grindstone church. Your friendship, leadership, and example make everyday enriching and exciting. Your influence on my life, thinking, and writing cannot be quantified. Thank you for inspiring me to be a better leader and better disciple.

Thanks to the emerging leaders at Grindstone church who continually inspire me to follow Jesus more passionately and authentically. Your fingerprints are all over this book, because I've learned just as much from you as you've learned from me. My times with you are some of my most treasured, and it's a pleasure to learn with and from you.

Thanks to Grindstone church for being such a special community to be a part of. I honestly can't imagine my life without Grindstone. It's a privilege and gift to serve Jesus with you.

Thanks to my wife Heather for leading by example. God continually uses your courage, love, and faith to inspire and teach me. Thanks for all of the encouragement and support. You are my best friend and there is nothing mere about my love for you.

introduction

The glory of God is a person fully alive.
~ St. Irenaeus

I believe that most of the time all God needs from us is honesty. Once He gets that, He's able to do to the rest.

I hope this book is honest. I want it to reflect part of myself and my journey thus far, but also point to places I believe God is leading me into. That means it's not a book written by a professional or expert. I'm still playing catch-up to many of the thoughts and ideas contained in this book. Those who know me well know that I'm a work-in-progress, but I'm in progress nonetheless. The good news is Jesus is the one orchestrating the progression.

The window between the ages of 18-25 is full of progression, and is one of the most formative stages of our lives. We experience growth throughout our lives, with each stage presenting new challenges and opportunities, but most people I know admit that these seven years are amongst the most powerful and soul-shaping. That's because a number of factors come together to form a perfect storm that ignites a quest; a spiritual expedition bent on working through theological and philosophical questions in ways that no other stage of life affords. It's often during these years that the following questions become urgent to resolve:

"What makes me different from my family or the people around me?"
"Am I lovable and am I capable of loving someone else?"
"Does God really love me?"
"Does God really like me?"
"What will I do with my life?"
"Do I matter?"
"Do I have something to contribute to this world that is of value?"

It's not that these questions are necessarily new (we've asked many of them before), but what makes the questions different is the new vantage point we are exploring them from. The questions haven't changed dramatically from earlier years, but *we have.* Socially, spiritually, physically, emotionally, psychologically, intellectually, experientially, etc., our world is enlarging at an almost unmanageable pace. The result is a kind of existential vertigo—a dizzying sense of confusion surrounding what has been, what is, and what is taking shape. During this time we often search for clarity on the four primary worldview questions:

1. "Who am I?"
2. "Where am I?"
3. "What's the problem?"
4. "What's the solution?"

These questions drive us to confront larger issues of identity, personal purpose, and meaning. Getting clarity on these issues is challenging, however, because at the same time we're bombarded by a myriad of voices offering advice, options, and opportunities—many of which are hollow and hopeless. We get distracted and derailed, and after a while it's easy to feel as if we're just treading water, drifting in a sea of questions, potentialities, and uncertainties.

Adding to the complexity is the deconstructive movement that often emerges during this time as well. Many of us begin to seriously question our faith, or walk away from it altogether. We unearth serious doubts and suspicions, and find that the black-and-white answers of our childhood and the glib answers of early adolescence don't help us cope with the growing realization that the world is much more complex than first imagined. While the teenage years are often a time of *physical* rebellion (e.g., sex, drugs, drinking, etc.), now a kind of *psychological/ philosophical* rebellion begins to take hold. In almost every area of our lives we're asking what really matters and why. We're beginning to wonder if our lives are the result of our own intentional choices or the result of choices made for us.

This is the time in our lives when all of the struggles, all of the questions, all of the anxieties and uncertainties need to become *secondary* to Jesus' call of discipleship. It's not that the struggles and questions we face are unimportant, it's that they're *so* important that to refuse to ground them in the person and power of Jesus is reckless. Trying to figure out life on our own sounds heroic to some, but we don't hold the answers to what we're dealing with: Jesus does. We can run from that truth, but we need to know that if we do we're running down a dead-end road.

Many people have chosen that road, but Jesus offers us a different one:

> *"Enter through the narrow gate. For wide is the gate and broad is the road that leads to destruction, and many enter through it. But small is the gate and narrow the road that leads to life, and only a few find it."* (Matthew 7:13-14)

Two roads: one goes to all the places that don't matter while the other goes to the only places that do. The choice Jesus is highlighting here isn't between heaven or hell, but discipleship to himself or idolatry. *Discipleship is the narrow road*, and only a few enter through it. It's hard, and it will cost us everything, but in exchange God will give us *His* everything. That's not a bad exchange, and in our most honest moments I think that is what we're all longing for.

Becoming Fully Alive

This book is divided into three parts.

Part I: Foundations explores the worldview foundations that need to be adopted in order for genuine discipleship to take root in our lives. These chapters examine the intersection between theology and philosophy, and how our assumptions surrounding each need to be examined and questioned if we want to see our lives transformed by Jesus' grace and power.

Part II: Money, Sex, and Power offers advice on dealing with the three great idols of money, sex, and power, and how discipleship to Jesus can redeem and transform our relationship to each.

Part III: Into the Kingdom focuses on creating a plan for daily discipleship, providing the tools and strategies needed to make discipleship to Jesus a lived reality.

"The glory of God is a person fully alive." This quote from St. Irenaeus is one of my favourites, because for me it captures the essence of the Christian faith perfectly. Genuine, real relationship with Jesus makes us *fully alive*—to God, ourselves, each other, and the world. That's what emerges from our lives if we choose to walk the narrow path of discipleship. Discipleship is the path Jesus uses to set us free; free from what limits, distorts, ensnares, and poisons us. It's not an easy path, but it's worth it.

As we begin this spiritual expedition together, I hope Paul's words to a young disciple will inspire and challenge us to take the next step with boldness and faith.

> *"Do not let anyone treat you as if you are unimportant because you are young. Instead, be an example to the believers with your words, your actions, your love, your faith, and your pure life."* (1 Timothy 4:12, NCV)

PART I foundations

1 in his dust

Come, follow me
~ Jesus, Matthew 4:19

Following Jesus is difficult. I understand why, at some point, all of us think about giving up. I understand why some do more than think about it. What Jesus calls us to do and become cannot be achieved casually or half-heartedly. I know because I've tried.

It wasn't long ago that I was engaged in a casual relationship with Jesus. I was interested in following Jesus to the extent it would benefit me socially, spiritually, economically, and emotionally. Any teachings of Jesus that didn't seem to hold an immediate promise or benefit for me were quickly filed into the optional category of my Christian life. Although I would have described myself as Christ-centred, Jesus was really just a *part* of my life; an accessory that was wonderful and helpful and made my life better. I guess I thought of Jesus as an upgrade to my life's operating system, and expected him to make things run smoother and more efficiently. I remember confidently claiming Jesus as my Lord and Saviour, scarcely knowing what those titles meant or implied. I used the terms "Christian," "disciple," and "believer" like slogans you'd find on a bumper sticker or fridge magnet. In the words of Brian McLaren: Jesus was more like my mascot than my Master.[1]

Looking back I cringe at how I approached my faith in its early stages. I started off with selfishness and arrogance, possessing little humility and even less wisdom. But maybe that's where I needed to start. Maybe that's where we all need to start. And maybe God is comfortable starting us there, as long as we don't linger for too long.

My confession, however, is that I did linger in that immature and complacent state much longer than I should have. But then something happened that changed everything. I'm not sure how it happened, or even exactly when it happened, but in my late teens I remember having a growing sense that I was being transitioned beyond a casual relationship with Jesus. This suspicion evolved into a conviction, and I began to realize that this was going to mean something more than Jesus as my mascot. God had placed a longing inside of me for something more substantial and real than half-hearted Christianity could deliver.

"I want to know Christ and the power of his resurrection and the fellowship of sharing in his sufferings, becoming like him" (Philippians

---

1 *A Generous Orthodoxy* (Zondervan, 2004), p. 88.

3:10). Those were Paul's words, but in a real sense they were becoming my own. That longing became a new journey for me and my relationship with Jesus. Slowly but noticeably I was being changed from the inside out, and I found myself eager and excited to embrace all of Jesus' teachings, not just the stuff that sounded good to my ego-driven self. My understanding of myself, others, the world, and Jesus began to enlarge in ways that made it impossible to continue living a self-centred Christian life. Increasingly I felt as if I was being swept up into something bigger than myself; a larger story of which my life was becoming a part.

I think this book is meant to be a guide for those who feel like God is building a similar momentum within their own lives. Maybe you haven't been able to articulate your inner experience precisely, but you've sensed that God is up to something big, and you're being pulled into it. My advice to you: don't resist it. I know it's scary to let go of what you've known and move into a "new land," but don't let fear get the better of you. I think it is during these points of transition that many people turn away from Jesus out of the uncertainty they're experiencing. But you must find your courage. As you move forward God will cause your desire for Christ to eclipse whatever has been holding you back from following Jesus in a deeper way. And at that moment you'll be ready to be born again... again.

You will be ready for discipleship.

Follower or Disciple?

Discipleship is not for the faint of heart. It's the hardest thing we'll ever enter into. That's because discipleship means more than just believing in theological concepts, and it means more than just ramping up our commitment to church attendance, bible study, or volunteerism. Discipleship is like entering into an apprenticeship where in a moment-by-moment process we're slowly becoming like the master we're learning under. To be a disciple of Jesus, therefore, is to commit ourselves into an apprenticeship to Jesus. That apprenticeship starts the moment we begin to take seriously the two things Jesus said were the most important things to him: loving God with every fibre of our being, and treating others like we'd like to be treated (Mark 12:30-31). That's what a disciple of Jesus is trying to chase down. That's what a disciple is committed to living out in the muck and mire of everyday life—at school, at work, at home, at play.

But not everyone who follows Jesus is chasing this same goal. People follow Jesus for all kinds of reasons, and that's why I see a distinction made within the gospels between two groups associated with Jesus: the *crowds* who *followed* Jesus[2] and Jesus' *disciples*[3]. Many think of these groups as one and the same, using the terms *follower* and *disciple* as synonyms. This is perpetuated within Christian circles as these terms are often used interchangeably (e.g., "I'm a disciple of Jesus/I'm a follower of Christ"). I used to see things that way myself, flippantly attaching both terms to my journey as a Christian. But today a new picture is emerging of what it

---

2 Matthew 4:25; Luke 9:11.
3 Matthew 8:23; Mark 6:41; John 4:27.

meant to be a *disciple* in Jesus' day[4], and these insights have encouraged and challenged me in ways that have transformed my life. Because of these insights I'm now convinced that it neither helpful nor biblical to collapse the terms *follower* and *disciple* together. I think the writers of the gospels gave us this distinction for a reason.

Lots of people followed Jesus. Anyone could follow Jesus, and if anyone did they became part of the nebulous mass of people known as *the crowds*, or *followers*. But the designation of *disciple* meant you were following Jesus in a more intentional way. It meant that you were in an apprenticeship to Jesus; an intensified relationship that was neither casual nor half-hearted.

One reason the New Testament writers made a distinction between *followers* and *disciples* (e.g., Matthew 5:1) was that in the 1st century discipleship was a status achieved by very few. An elaborate educational system had been established by the Jewish community in order to identify and empower the best and brightest students of the Scriptures. From childhood onward young boys (and within certain regions young girls) were given a regimented course of instruction and memorization centred on the Scriptures. Those who excelled and showed promise would graduate to more intense study. Each level was more challenging than the next, and this demanding progression purged all but the most exceptional students. Those who remained were deemed

---

4 I am immeasurably indebted to the monumental efforts of Ray Vander Laan and his tireless research in understanding the historical context of 1st century Judaism and early Christianity (www.followtherabbi.com).

worthy of the opportunity to seek out an established rabbi (usually aged 30 and over) and make a request to enter into a discipleship relationship with him.

However, being the brightest and the best could not guarantee someone a spot within the inner circle of a revered rabbi. Excelling through each level of education only gave the student permission to approach a rabbi whom they deeply respected and *ask* if they could become their disciple. A rabbi would then take time to test the student in order to evaluate whether they had what it took to enter the way of discipleship. What were rabbis looking for during this time of testing?

First, a student had to display mastery of the biblical text. As a starting point, a rabbi would expect that the student had memorized the Scriptures by heart. This would need to be coupled with a special ability to engage in sophisticated discussions around interpretation and application of the Torah as well.[5]

Second, a rabbi would not take on the student as a disciple unless they displayed a pervasive passion for God and His kingdom. Like modern teachers today ancient rabbis knew that passion was often what separated great students from good ones. The rabbi, therefore, would spend time with the student in order to make sure they possessed the fire and *chutzpah*[6] necessary for discipleship.

---

5 This fact is all the more impressive due to the fact that at this point many of the candidates were around 15 years of age!

6 *Chutzpah* is a Jewish term that roughly equates to having a "daring boldness." Today we might use expressions like "She's got guts!" or "He's pretty ballsy!" to convey the same idea.

Finally, a rabbi would expect the student to possess a genuine love for his community and the Jewish traditions. A rabbi would not accept a student who was brilliant and passionate, but didn't value living out their faith within the broader community of believers. This was because all rabbis expected a commitment to community to be a core value for would-be disciples.

Text. Passion. Community. Those were the foundations of discipleship in Jesus' world.[7] Excelling in all of these areas was an extremely demanding task, *but without all three qualities a rabbi would pass on potential candidates.* The calling of discipleship was simply too tough and too important to be left to those deemed "good enough." Only the best of the best could earn the right to be called a disciple.

Why would someone in the 1st century go through all this effort just to be *considered* for discipleship? The answer might come as a surprise to those of us who would only make such efforts if monetary reward was the possible payoff at the end of the process. Potential disciples were motivated by the promise of a reward, but it wasn't monetary or material in nature. They worked, studied, and passionately pursued the rabbi because their goal was to become one of the great rabbis! The Hebrew people didn't seek to emulate the rich or the politically powerful (those whom their pagan neighbours idolized). Instead, they sought to be shaped by those who possessed deep wisdom and insight emerging out of a robust and intimate relationship with God.

So each and every disciple was involved in an intense apprenticeship

7 That The World May Know Ministries (2005). *In the Dust of the Rabbi: becoming a disciple.*

with their rabbi. But a follower wasn't bound by such expectations and could participate in a more casual association. They could follow from a distance and could take and leave elements of the rabbi's teaching and lifestyle as they saw fit. But a disciple could not do this. Why? Because a disciple did not *want* to do this! A disciple was committed to something more than just an informal connection with the rabbi—they were consumed by the desire to become like the rabbi they followed! Today we think of a good student as someone who wants to know what the teacher knows, but a disciple was someone who wanted to *become like the teacher.* That meant if something was important to the rabbi, it became important to his disciples.

When I first learned all of this, I was overwhelmed. Against such expectations, how could I call myself a disciple? *Mastery of the Text?* I hadn't even *read* the whole Bible, yet alone memorized it. *Commitment to community?* I thought of myself as a good friend, but knew that community meant something much more sacrificial in Jesus' day than I was living out. *Passion for God and His kingdom?* I guess I felt this way *some* of the time.

If these three criteria formed the only lens through which to evaluate ourselves, who would dare claim the title of *disciple?* Personally, I didn't come close to qualifying for discipleship based on these criteria.

But then I learned that none of Jesus' original disciples did either. I learned that for Jesus the status of disciple was not *earned,* but *given.* Jesus discarded the traditional assumptions and expectations of the rabbinic schools around him. His school of discipleship was revolutionary, unexpected, and audacious in its practice. Notice that in stark contrast to the traditional rabbinic pattern, Jesus didn't pick the best of the best. Two disciples, James and John, are identified in the Bible as fishermen. Translation: they weren't the A+ students. They hadn't made the grade and been counted worthy of discipleship by the established system. They lacked something the rabbis of the day saw as necessary to enter into discipleship. They weren't the elite, and that meant they weren't good enough to become anyone's disciple. But that didn't matter to Jesus. Jesus saw something in them that the world—*even the religious world*—missed. He saw within James and John a potential that they didn't even see in themselves.

And notice that Jesus chose *them*! In fact, *none* of the disciples listed in the gospels approached Jesus and asked to become his disciple. Why? *Because none of them would have assumed they were good enough to be a disciple!* They were the C+ students in school. They weren't the valedictorians or all-stars—but Jesus called them anyway. And continues to today.

Think about that. "Come and follow me" isn't just an invitation to them; it's also an invitation to you. And you're not being called because you're the best and brightest that the world has to offer (far from it—1 Corinthians 1:7!). You're being called and chosen because Jesus sees something in you that you may not even see in yourself. He honestly, deeply, passionately believes that you can become like him! He wants you to be more than a casual follower who is part of the crowd. He wants you to become his *disciple* and be a part of his mission to reshape the world through his power. The rest of the world may dismiss you as insignificant in the grand scheme of things, but Jesus believes in you and has plans to use you in extraordinary ways.

How Dirty Are You?

There is an ancient Jewish proverb that states: "Follow a rabbi, drink in his words, and be covered by the dust from his feet." It's said that you could tell who the rabbi's disciples were because they were the dirtiest members of his entourage. They wanted to get as close as possible to their rabbi in the hope that his wisdom, knowledge, kindness, and courage would rub off on them. In fact, they would often follow so closely that over time they would find themselves covered in the dust that was kicked up from the rabbi's steps as the group travelled along the countryside.

So how dirty are you? As I've read and reflected on the distinction between being a follower and being a disciple, I keep coming back to the same conclusion: the essential difference between the two groups relates to their *proximity* to Jesus. Followers trail Jesus from whatever distance makes them comfortable. Disciples follow Jesus as closely as possible. They want to get dirty and be covered in his dust in hopes that Jesus' priorities, values, power, and character will rub off on them and change them forever.

I want to be the dirtiest Christian I can be. I want to be covered in his dust and I want Jesus to shape me into my truest self in him. Then I want him to use me in whatever way he sees fit to help bring restoration and healing to this broken world through his power. This passion fuels me to continually learn more about what it means to follow Jesus as a disciple. And it's so encouraging to remember that Jesus doesn't expect or need me to be the best of the best; he simply needs me to passionately want to be a disciple who's willing to be used by him for his glory.

In His Dust

I've wrestled with getting a tattoo for a long time. It's one of those things that I've been cautious to rush into, because the world is littered with people who thought a dolphin or Star Wars tattoo was an awesome idea at the time. I'm not against tattoos; I'm just against stupid ones. I think if you're going to get one it better be something very meaningful and timeless—a reflection of who you are and who you are becoming. While I haven't taken the dive yet, I find myself coming back to the following tattoo idea:

It's the Hebrew word *aphar* and it means *dust*. It has come to hold deep significance for me on many levels. It is the same word that is used in Genesis 2:7 as God creates Adam from the dust of the ground, and serves as a reminder of my finiteness and need for God's breath of life in order to be fully alive. It is used in Deuteronomy 9:21 to describe the dust that is left over as a result of God's destruction of Israel's idols, and serves as a reminder that God loves me enough to destroy the things in my life that only offer empty promises and hollow hope. It is used in 1 Samuel 2:8 to affirm that God "raises the poor from the dust" and serves as a reminder to me that those who find themselves broken and crushed can find a hope in Him that can't be found anywhere else.

But the main reason I'm considering this Hebrew word as a tattoo is that whenever I see it I'm reminded of my primary calling to be covered in Jesus' dust as I follow him passionately and closely. It helps me remember the commitment I've made to get as dirty as possible as a *disciple*, and in the process leave half-hearted Christianity behind.

I realize now that anyone can follow Jesus, but not everyone has the drive to be a disciple. Relatively speaking, being a follower is so much easier and convenient than setting out on the journey of discipleship. That's probably why lots of Christians are content to be followers. Frankly, if that's where you find yourself as you read this, then I'm not sure how impactful the rest of this book will be for you. I won't be spending time trying to convince you to be a disciple through manipulation or hype. I think convincing and conviction are works of the Spirit. All I offer is some help in understanding what being a disciple may mean for your life, if that's the road you want to take. I hope it's the road you will take, because the richest and most extraordinary experiences in life are reserved for those who decide to follow Jesus as disciples.

Two thousand years ago a bunch of nobodies were given the chance to become disciples to the world's greatest rabbi, and were invited to be part of God's plan to rescue a broken world. I wonder if, right before they were called, they had the same longings and stirrings within them that you have inside. I wonder if they could have ever imagined how their lives would be transformed as they courageously responded to Jesus' call to become disciples. We know this much: they were never the same after accepting Jesus' invitation, and neither was the world in which they lived.

Today that same rabbi is calling you. He's not calling you to casually believe in him. He's not calling you to casually follow him. He's calling you to become his *disciple*. This is your time. Today Jesus is inviting you to step into something more beautiful and profound than you could possibly imagine.

I hope you'll say yes. Because if you do, you will never be the same, and neither will the world in which you live.

2 the transforming vision

For every thousand hacking at the leaves of evil,
there is one striking at the root.

~ Henry David Thoreau

The challenges we will encounter as disciples are numerous. However, the greatest obstacle to discipleship may not be what we would assume. When I ask people what the most significant challenge to faithfully following Jesus is, specific sins and temptations inevitably rise to the surface. I don't doubt how much these particular challenges shape the discipleship journey of those I talk to, but the things that pose the greatest threat to us are rarely the things that are most obvious—the "hot sins" (to borrow a phrase of Richard Rohr's) that confront us and entice us. Through my own journey of discipleship I'm learning that the greatest struggles have less to do with the things of this world and more to do with how I *see* the world.

All of us live our lives through a specific *worldview*, which acts like a pair of glasses through which we see and interpret our world. Our worldview is made up of our assumptions, expectations, experiences, and knowledge. It includes everything from our views on fashion to morality to the role of government. Much of the time we are unaware of our worldview, and we often mistakenly assume we're seeing things the way they are; that our view is the correct one. That's why we all need to step back and make sure that the glasses we're looking through are helping us to see clearly and not distorting our view of reality. If the worldview we hold to doesn't help us see reality with clarity and precision, we'll find ourselves on a spiritual journey that parallels the children of Israel in the desert: years of wandering with no progress.

Does that feel like your experience of following Jesus sometimes? You've tried hard, but no matter what you do it feels like you're going in circles and failing to make any progress? You're not alone. Moving into my twenties I was sincere, I was dedicated and I wanted to follow Jesus intentionally. But I was like someone who had been given a terribly inaccurate lens through which to see the world and my calling as a disciple within it. I quickly came to the realization that if I didn't get new glasses, working harder wasn't going to make much difference.

If someone was trying to get from point A to point B within a city, but they had impaired vision due to a bad prescription lens, driving faster would hardly be helpful. They'd just get lost faster! Being positive and staying hopeful wouldn't make much difference either. They'd just be the most pleasant, visually impaired lost person on the road!

The solutions to the problems that confront us don't necessarily come with trying harder, staying positive, or having more faith. The solutions need to start with finding a pair of glasses that allows us to see things clearly and accurately. If we try to act differently without learning to *see* differently, we'll be fighting an uphill battle. But if we first try to *see* things differently, new behaviours will naturally follow.

But how do we change our glasses—how do we change our worldview? We can't. Most of the time a change in worldview is something that is done *to us*. It comes during a time when we see, hear, learn, or experience something which is so at odds with our assumed understanding of the world, that we are jolted into a new way of seeing. Whatever the event or encounter is that causes us to see things differently, the effect is called a *paradigm shift*. A paradigm is the way we see and understand something. It's another way of talking about the glasses through which we see the world.

One of the most significant and far-reaching paradigm shifts in my life occurred during my first year at Redeemer University College. As an 18 year old who had been a Christian for four years, I was almost completely unaware of the worldview through which I was trying to understand reality and follow Jesus; a worldview that was deeply flawed and full of untruths. I needed a new prescription—a new set of worldview glasses that enabled me to see reality clearly and accurately if I was going to follow Jesus in a way that was transformative. And I got them.

In a small classroom full of people I did not know, my professor of worldview studies Michael W. Goheen proceeded to lead our class through a history of Christian theology and philosophy. Those Wednesday afternoon classes were some of the most powerful of my university career, because they opened my eyes to what I have come to believe is *the* most significant enemy to genuine biblical faith and discipleship.

A Brief History of the Western Worldview

Once upon a time there was a man named Plato. Plato was a revered Greek philosopher who was the understudy of Socrates, considered by many to be one of the most influential thinkers ever. Plato was no slouch himself. His ideas about the nature of reality would shape human thought and much of Western civilization for thousands of years.

Plato was a dualist. That means he believed that reality was composed of two (dual) parts. Plato came to call these two parts the world of *forms* and the world of *matter*. For Plato these two dimensions of reality could be differentiated based on whether the aspects of reality found in each were *eternal* (existing forever) or *finite* (existing for only a period of time). The world of *forms* was the invisible, immaterial, and eternal part of reality. The world of *matter* was the visible, material, and finite part of reality. Because the world of *forms* contained those things which were eternal (e.g., ideas, concepts, thoughts, the gods, etc.), Plato came to promote this world as superior to the world of *matter*. The world of *matter*, after all, consisted of things that would eventually decay and cease to exist (e.g., plants, animals, the human body, etc.).

Plato used the human being as a living embodiment of his concept of a universal dualism, teaching that humans were composed of an invisible, eternal, "higher" immaterial *mind* and a visible, finite, "lower" physical *body*. These two aspects were considered relatively separate and distinct for Plato (and subsequent Greek philosophers), and Plato's mind/body dualism became a popular way of understanding the nature of both humanity and the larger universe.

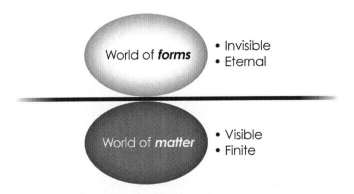

From here, Plato took his model and began to plot which activities of life belonged where. For each activity, Plato asked whether it belonged to the higher world of the mind or the lower world of the body. Through this process Plato would come to place all human activity either "above the line" or "below the line." Activities associated with the mind were celebrated and promoted, while those associated with the body were discouraged and shamed. For example, activities like philosophy and education were given a place "above the line" because Plato viewed these as being rooted in ideas (which belonged to the eternal and invisible world of *forms*). Activities like farming, sex, and physical fitness were placed "below the line" because they were rooted in acts of the body which belonged to the finite and material world of *matter*, and were therefore seen as inferior uses of one's energy and talents.

Plato's counsel to all who would listen was to pursue a life that was absorbed in the world of *forms* (i.e., the *mind*). Why? Because Plato's worldview assumed activities within this dimension of reality were the higher, eternal ones that held true significance. To spend time participating in the world of *matter* was to squander one's life away. Why spend one's life investing in things that will perish when one can invest in things that are eternal and incorruptible? Plato's worldview led to a general assumption that doing anything connected with material reality was a second class option; one that was rarely valuable or legitimate in one's development as a human being.

Plato's dualistic worldview became immensely popular. Many people adopted it as their worldview and took Plato's counsel seriously. Plato's dualism underwent many evolutions and even faced significant opposition,[8] but the basic framework which Plato laid out for describing reality stood the test of time and continued to shape the development of human thought in relatively unhindered ways.

One of the interesting things to note is that some of Christianity's most significant theologians and thinkers were heavily influenced by Plato's thought. Two of the most influential Christian theologians, St. Augustine

---

8 Plato's understudy Aristotle argued that the world of *matter* was superior to the world of *forms*.

and Thomas Aquinas, were sincere and devoted disciples of Jesus who serve as examples here. After coming to faith they sought to provide would-be disciples with an accurate worldview rooted in the Bible that would promote faithfulness to Christ and his mission. However, despite their attempts to ground their ideas in the revealed truths of Scripture, Augustine and Aquinas (albeit in different ways) integrated foundational elements of Plato's dualism into their thinking. Both of these thinkers were unable to discern the full extent to which Platonic dualism had shaped their *own* worldview assumptions, and the result was the creation of a worldview mash-up that combined Plato's ideas and Biblical truths.

A Christian Dualism

The outworking of this collision between Plato's dualism and the revelation of Scripture was that Plato's higher world of *forms* was replaced with the *sacred* dimension of reality, while the lower world of *matter* became the repository for all things *secular*. Then, using the Bible as their guide, Augustine and Aquinas divided elements of reality into either the *sacred* or *secular* category, all the while believing this would promote discipleship and strengthen the faith of those they taught. The result: a Christian dualistic worldview that was little more than a remixed version of Plato's dualism.

What was the essential message of this Christianized version of Plato's worldview? Almost the same as Plato's: spend your life doing things "above the line" and avoid things "below the line" and you will experience transformation and spiritual growth. This made the call of discipleship pretty straightforward, because all you needed to do was busy yourself with *sacred* (i.e., heavenly/holy) activities while avoiding *secular* (i.e., worldly/sinful) ones.

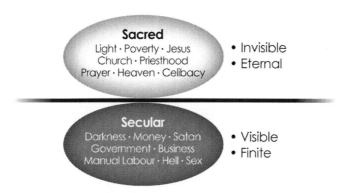

"So what?" you're thinking. "The Bible talks about spiritual things and unspiritual things. I don't see the problem with this way of seeing reality."

Exactly. That's the point. *The things that pose the greatest threat to us are rarely the things that are obvious.* What makes this worldview so dangerous is that it *sounds* biblical because it uses biblical themes, terms, and ideas. But cults do the same thing, and there's nothing truthful, good, or genuinely biblical about cults. Just because something *sounds* Christian or biblical, doesn't mean it is.

Which brings me to my major point: I believe the greatest obstacle to following Jesus as a disciple is this Christian dualistic worldview.

Actually, it's not Christian at all, and I will therefore be using the term *dualism* when referring to it from this point forward.

This dualistic worldview is not a *slightly* inaccurate prescription lens, but a *completely distorted one.* It's not enough to call it a faulty paradigm; dualism is a deeply anti-Christian way of seeing and understanding reality. This assertion may seem strong, but this dualistic view is not compatible with a faith that is shaped by Scripture because it is built on two faulty assumptions:

1. Reality is composed of two separate worlds.
2. These worlds exist in opposition to each other; one being fundamentally good and the other fundamentally evil.

Notice the first assumption: reality is composed of two separate worlds. Really? I think there are different *dimensions* within God's creation, but no where in Scripture does it even come close to insinuating that the cosmos suffers from split personality disorder. Biblically speaking, reality is a unified and integrated creation of God (Genesis 1-2). While there are mysterious and unfathomable dimensions within creation, the Bible teaches us that all of these dimensions come together in ways that overlap and interlock, and do not exist as distinct worlds with absolute borders and boundaries.

Now notice the second assumption dualism makes: activities "above the line" (i.e., the *sacred* world of *forms/mind*) are *automatically* good, holy, and right, while things "below the line" (i.e., the *secular* world of *matter/body*) are *automatically* evil, unholy, and sinful. But is that the case? Is going to church *automatically* a holy and good activity? Is prayer *always* done in a way that is right and good? Is sex *always* a sinful act? Does my job as a pastor mean that I am *automatically* more Christ-like and holy than my neighbour who works as an electrician? The answer to all of these questions is, "Obviously not!" However, a dualistic worldview forces you to give a very different answer; it forces you to say, "Yes" to each of these questions.

Because of the assumptions dualism forces us to adopt, we need to reject it as unbiblical and deeply anti-Christian. A dualistic worldview—even a Christianized one—is not a worldview that allows us to see reality clearly in order to navigate it faithfully.

A Christian Dualist?

One of the ways we can identify whether or not we're viewing the world through dualistic glasses is to become aware of the assumptions we hold about life, God, spiritual growth, faith, etc. Some of the most common perspectives that reveal a dualistic worldview include:

Christians should only listen to Christian music. The assumption here is that Christian music, because it is written and produced by Christians and includes explicitly Christian lyrics, is holy and spiritual. It is "above the line" due to its "sacred" content. Conversely, any and all forms of music that are created by non-

Christians and do not possess explicitly Christian content are "worldly" and devoid of wisdom, beauty, spiritual insight, etc.

Pastors and missionaries are the most spiritual Christians. Whether or not this idea is explicitly stated, it's often assumed by many within churches. Why? Well, if we see through a dualistic lens, this assertion makes sense. The lives of pastors and missionaries are assumed to be full of holy activities like prayer, Bible study, ministering in Jesus' name, etc., and they are therefore assumed to have a higher "spiritual density" than other Christians (who follow Jesus, but whose lives are not dedicated to "spiritual activities").

The Bible is the only source of truth and wisdom. For those holding to a dualist paradigm, there is a deep suspicion attached to any insights that cannot be validated by a direct proof-text from the Bible. It is assumed that insights that come from non-biblical sources are automatically unspiritual, worldly, and sinful, so exposure to these ideas is foolish at best and dangerous at worst. Within such a view Christians can only trust knowledge emerging directly from the Bible (and perhaps only Christian interpretations of it).

Heaven is our home. Christians who see the world through a dualistic lens spend a lot of time thinking about their eternal destiny in heaven. By *heaven*, they usually assume somewhere far away from this world or reality as we know it. For them salvation in Jesus is freedom from sin that secures entrance into an eternal heavenly reality.

These are just some examples of the kind of thinking that can emerge if one holds to a dualistic worldview. You may hold to none, some, or all of them, but I hope you are beginning to see the connection between one's worldview and how one lives out their faith (or whether they do at all!).

Dualism is something a disciple of Jesus needs to confront and reject. Why? Because seeing the world through dualistic glasses will cause us to view Jesus as the Lord and Saviour of *parts* of our lives. If we hold to a dualism of any kind, we will automatically assume all things "Jesus" or "Christian" only hold significance for the "spiritual" parts of our lives (whatever we define those to be). We'll act like a Christian at church or in "spiritual" contexts, but we'll give little thought to what it means to be a disciple in our school classes or our part-time jobs. After all, aren't these the "non-spiritual" (i.e., secular) areas of our lives? A dualistic worldview encourages this line of thinking, and will prevent us from integrating our love and commitment to Jesus into every aspect of our lives. If we want to be disciples, therefore, we must be continually fighting against a dualistic view of reality.

At no point does Scripture teach dualism in any way, shape, or form. We need to be careful that we don't read a dualistic perspective *into*

Scripture, and instead come to the text with an awareness of how often dualistic assumptions colour everything we read there. We have to come with the courage and resolve necessary to form a biblical, anti-dualistic worldview. But what would such a worldview look like?

A Divine Conspiracy

In Genesis God created everything and declared His entire creation to be "very good" (Genesis 1:31). Notice that *everything* is deemed "very good"—not half of it or part of it or some of it. Immaterial, invisible aspects of God's creation are not "very good" while material, finite things are "very bad." Everything—the mind, the body, humans, animals, ideas, dirt, love, laughter, sex, trees, etc.—is declared by God as *very good*. The first chapter of Genesis provides us with a foundational component to a faithful biblical worldview: God's creation is not built upon a dualism of any kind.[9] God didn't make some parts of creation holy and others unholy. It's all beautiful, good, and pleasing to Him.

However, in the third chapter of Genesis we read that a corruption occurred that affected every square inch of God's creation. This corruption is called *sin*, and it distorts and perverts everything that God made as very good. The mind, the body, humans, animals, ideas, dirt, love, laughter, sex, trees, etc.—once pure and unpolluted are now all tainted by something that detracts from the glory of God's original design

---

9 It is interesting to note that the Jewish *Shema* includes the preface "The Lord our God; the Lord is *One*" (emphasis mine). This is in part a fiercely anti-dualistic affirmation of the unified and harmonious nature of both God and His creative activity.

and intent. Genesis chapter three provides us with another foundational component to a faithful biblical worldview: because of humanity's fall into sin, there is nothing in creation which is free from sin's corrupting influence.

So in the first three chapters of Genesis we are given two truths that help frame the parameters of a biblical worldview: Everything was created "very good" by God, but everything has been poisoned by the toxic influence of sin.

The final framing truth is revealed throughout the chapters following Genesis 3, as the rest of Scripture discloses God's mission to repair and restore His creation back to its unpolluted, "very good" condition. The word used to describe this process is *redemption*, and it underscores the fact that God has not given up on His creation. Despite our rejection of Him and our participation in the destruction and pollution of creation, God is energetically reclaiming His creation from the grip of sin, death, and destruction.

In stark contrast to Plato's dualistic foundations, the early chapters of the Bible provide us with three framing truths that come together to form a pair of glasses that enable us see reality clearly and accurately; a worldview that challenges our assumptions about what it means to navigate our world as humans and, more specifically, disciples of Jesus:

1. God created all things "very good."
2. Sin has corrupted all aspects of God's "very good" creation.
3. God is conspiring to rescue and restore all things through Jesus.

Once these assumptions begin to take root in our lives, our outlook on everything is rearranged. Our perspective changes from seeing things in good and bad or black-and-white categories, to something more complex and nuanced. We begin to recognize beauty in the broken, and the brokenness in beauty. We're overwhelmed to find out that instead of giving up on a world bent on self-destruction God is working to rescue the world through Jesus.

A biblical worldview helps us see that cutting through the "very good" nature of all things is this corruption called sin. The result is that things are not the way they are supposed to be. Our calling as disciples therefore, is to enter into all areas of life with the intention to *redirect them in God glorifying ways.*

Dualism makes things too easy. It assumes by just doing "spiritual/ sacred" things and avoiding "worldly/secular" things we will experience transformation in Christ. But that way of seeing won't get us very far, because the issue isn't whether we are above or below some arbitrary line, but in what *direction* we are moving: Are we engaging in sports, relationships, video games, school, business, etc., in a way that renews and reveals God's "very good" design? Or are we engaging in it in such a way that we are continuing to distort its "very good" nature through sinful and self-serving means?

"So whether you eat or drink or whatever you do, do it all for the glory of God" (1 Corinthians 10:31). Whatever we do: eating, studying, dating, landscaping, watching movies, flipping burgers, having sex, praying, playing video games, etc., *direct it* in a way that counters the influence of sin and aligns the act to God's wise and good intentions.

"Whatever you do... do it all for the glory of God." No one holding to a dualist view of the world could say that, because according to such a view there are things in life that one simply *cannot* do to the glory of God because they are *automatically* unholy. But Paul's worldview wasn't a dualistic one, which empowered him to offer a radically different vision for the Christian life.

Now there is some confusion at this point because Paul, more than any other Biblical author, uses some Greek philosophical terminology to make his points. But we need to see that these are appropriate accommodations because Paul had to communicate the truths of Scripture to a those heavily influenced by a Greek worldview. Therefore he was forced to use Greek language (and paradigms are *always* attached to language) as he taught about the gospel of Jesus. However, that does not mean that Paul *adopted* or *believed in* the dualism outlook his audience held to. In fact, Scriptures such as 1 Corinthians 10:31 give us a strong example of Paul's anti-dualistic worldview. Paul knew the created goodness in all things, but he was also aware of the ways that sin pulls the creation of God towards destructive ends (e.g., Romans 6:23). Instead of counselling the Corinthian church to avoid activities connected with the body and pleasure (such as eating and drinking), Paul challenged them to see that by *redirecting* these practices from destructive, sinful expressions to restorative, godly ones, they could bring glory and honour to God. That's why Paul didn't tell the Corinthian Christians to abandon their cultural traditions or practices altogether; he wanted them to learn what it meant to do these things in ways that glorified God and revealed His goodness.

So how does this biblical, non-dualistic worldview change the assumptions we looked at earlier? Let's revisit them and explore the difference wearing a different set of glasses can make.

Christians should only listen to Christian music. Because the creational goodness of God is inherent to all aspects of creation, we are free to expose ourselves to whatever is true, noble, right, pure, lovely, and admirable (Philippians 4:8). We may find that the explicitly biblical content of Christian artists encourages and shapes us in healthy ways, but we do not assume that this automatically happens simply because it is an explicitly Christian song. We also don't assume that even within explicitly non-Christian music redemptive themes cannot be found. Whatever the artist's religious affiliation (or lack thereof), someone committed to an anti-dualistic, biblical worldview will seek to embrace the excellent and praiseworthy while rejecting "every pretension that sets itself up against the knowledge of God" (2 Corinthians 10:5).

Pastors and missionaries are the most spiritual Christians. A biblical worldview challenges us to realize that being spiritual isn't a matter of what we do, but in *how and why we're doing it.* The most genuinely spiritual Christians are those who work at their job with all of their heart, "as working for the Lord, not for men" (Colossians 3:23). Therefore, the disciple trained in interior design that serves the needs of their client and brings the best of their creativity and passion to the table is more spiritual than the pastor who uses their Sunday morning platform to self-promote and fuel their egoistic need to be recognized and applauded.

The Bible is the only source of truth and wisdom. Disciples seek truth from *both* of God's revelations. They are open and eager to learn from God's *specific* revelation contained within Scripture, but are equally excited to embrace the truths found within God's *general* revelation of creation (which in the broadest sense includes the insights and contributions of others in the fields of biology, psychology, history, physics, etc., and not just what we think of as *nature*). While the Bible is the foundational bedrock of a disciple's understanding of the world, Proverbs 1:20 tells us that "Wisdom calls aloud in the street, she raises her voice in the public squares." This is the Bible's way of affirming the view that there are "books in the running brooks, sermons in stones, and good in everything."[10] This posture towards reality allows those with a biblical, non-dualistic worldview to fearlessly explore truth and open themselves up to any insight that has been "received with thanksgiving, because it is consecrated by the word of God and prayer" (1 Timothy 4:4-5). From this perspective, *all* dimensions of learning and truth seeking become an act of worship, not just those done within the margins of Scripture.

Heaven is my home. Someone viewing reality through a dualistic lens may assume that at the end of all things God will destroy physical matter and sweep up the faithful into an immaterial, eternal future in heaven. But such a dualistic conception flies in the face of the final chapters of Revelation, where we are continually confronted by the assertion that God is not going to throw away His world. His plan is to redeem and restore it, and eventually return to dwell within it forever. Notice what John records in Revelation 21:

---

10 Duke Senior, *As You Like It*, (Act 2 scene 1).

"Then I saw a new heaven and a new earth, for the first heaven and the first earth had passed away, and there was no longer any sea. I saw the Holy City, the new Jerusalem, coming down out of heaven from God, prepared as a bride beautifully dressed for her husband. And I heard a loud voice from the throne saying, 'Now the dwelling of God is with men, and he will live with them'." (Revelation 21:1-3)

In John's vision heaven and earth become one![11] Heaven is *not* our final destiny. We are going to live forever in a real, material, perfected world that parallels our experience here and now, except that "There will be no more death or mourning or crying or pain, for the old order of things has passed away" (Revelation 21:4). This makes sense, however, if the material world in which we live is not inferior (as Plato taught) and is instead something important that God wants to sustain forever.

A New Kind of Christian

For too long Plato's dualistic worldview has impeded Christians' ability to live out their calling faithfully. Dualism has been subtly legitimating the idea that Christians should take Jesus as Lord and Saviour of their "spiritual" lives while doing whatever they please with the rest of their lives.

---

11 cf. Isaiah 65:17-25.

It's time to reject this way of seeing reality—this inaccurate worldview lens—and replace it with one that is simultaneously more challenging and biblical. It's time for a new kind of Christian to emerge who sees reality clearly and serves Jesus faithfully. It's time for a new kind of Christian to emerge who embraces Jesus as the Lord and Saviour of their *entire* lives. It's time for a new kind of Christian to emerge who boldly announces that there is a divine conspiracy taking place that will not rest until heaven and earth are one, and creation is restored.

The Bible offers us a powerful, transforming vision that shows us how to experience all things in Him. The Scriptures help us to see clearly so we can make real progress in our growth as disciples. Let's not settle for the vision we've inherited from Plato; a distorted worldview that muddles our vision, fractures our allegiance to Jesus, and leaves us wandering aimlessly as disciples.

3 wild beasts and angels

And Jesus was there in the wilderness forty days, tempted of Satan; and was with the wild beasts; and the angels ministered unto him.

~ Mark 1:13 (KJV)

Have you ever really struggled with your faith? I mean really, *really* dug deep and asked some hard questions about what it all means? If you have then I commend you, because I know how difficult that process is. It takes a lot of guts to initiate that journey and even more fortitude to stick it out. It's a lot easier to go into autopilot and mindlessly trust that what you know and believe is true. But if you want to serve Jesus authentically and faithfully, struggling through elements of your faith will be necessary.

As a disciple you'll always need to fight the temptation to follow Jesus vicariously through other people's discipleship journey. This happens when, instead of reading and studying the Bible ourselves, we only read *other people's* reflections on the Bible. Or it can happen when we hear and celebrate how *others* encounter God as they serve the marginalized and poor, but never bother to lift a finger ourselves. Discipleship to Jesus is an intensely personal calling, and one that you can't outsource. If you do, you'll end up with a second-hand faith and a second-hand experience of God.

To move into a first-hand experience of God, we need to adopt an exciting and dangerous practice that will force us to struggle in fresh ways with our faith. This practice is exciting because, if we step into it with courage and resolve, our faith will genuinely be transformed, and we'll come to a place where we'll *know* the truth that sets us free. But it's dangerous for the same reason. It will threaten our certainties—the things we may have assumed are obvious and the ideas we've placed total trust in. The practice I'm referring to often creates doubts, because it raises more questions than answers. It will push you into places you would rather not go.

I'm talking about the process of *deconstruction*. For those unfamiliar with the term, deconstruction is the method of critically analyzing something in order to expose unquestioned assumptions or internal contradictions. Stated even more literally, it means to take something apart (de-construct) in order to understand it in a new way. Deconstruction is ultimately about asking hard questions about what we believe and why. It questions everything within our worldview in order to ensure that we're building our lives on rock and not sand (Matthew 7:24-27).

Sometimes deconstruction gets a bad rap because it's seen as little more than an exercise in negativity, suspicion, and disbelief. But my experience is that when deconstruction is done out of a love for God and a passion to unearth His truth, it's incredibly valuable and faith building.

Deconstruction demands that we continually examine the core concepts we've built our faith on and ask, "What assumptions have coloured my understanding of these ideas? What has been the result? Are those assumptions accurate and biblical?" Through questions like these we begin to realize that we often read the Bible not as *it is*, but as *we are*, and this insight often opens up new and fresh ways of exploring the Scriptures. If done thoroughly and courageously, deconstruction allows us to encounter the Bible and our faith again for the first time.

Into the Desert

Almost at the very start of Mark's gospel, Jesus is led by the Spirit into the desert where he stays for forty days being tempted by the devil. The King James translation notes that Jesus was "with the wild beasts; and the angels ministered to him." For me, that entire scene stands as the perfect metaphor for the practice and process of godly deconstruction.

Deconstruction begins when we are led by the Spirit out of the familiar, into the "desert"—the place where we feel isolated and alone. When people begin asking the difficult questions and begin wrestling with their faith, they often have the sense that they are embarking on a lonely journey. That journey isn't quick and easy either. Jesus spends forty days in the desert, which for me points to the fact that the desert experience of deconstruction doesn't happen overnight. It often overlaps with several seasons within a person's life. It's a process, not an event.

During his time in the desert, Satan tempted Jesus in three ways:

1. Satan suggested that Jesus use his power transform stones into bread to avoid starvation.
2. Satan suggested that Jesus perform a miraculous act in order to show that he was the Son of God.
3. Satan invited Jesus to worship him and, in exchange, gain all the kingdoms of the world.

Notice that everything Jesus was tempted by was a good thing! Jesus using his power to avoid starving is not a bad thing. Jesus proving he's God's Son through a miracle isn't a bad thing. Jesus gaining control of all the kingdoms of the world isn't a bad thing.

So why are these temptations? Why would Jesus have sinned if he had done any of them? *Because what was being offered to Jesus was a shortcut.* Everything Satan tempted Jesus with, God was already going to provide to Jesus—*just not immediately.* This is an important insight, because it reveals that much of the time Satan tempts us with good things at the wrong time. Most of the time, the wrong time that we're being tempted by is *right now!* The point here is that Jesus resisted the temptation to take any short-cuts, and instead allowed the process to take its course. We have to do the same when it comes to deconstruction. Deconstruction is the exact opposite of the quick-fix and instant solution. That's why most people won't enter into it deeply.

The temptation to get easy, immediate answers is powerful for us, and we often give in to what is easy instead of sticking things out. The result of this decision, however, is always a superficial, second-hand faith. When it comes to our spiritual growth in Jesus, no one else can do the work for us. We need to put in our own blood, sweat, and tears. Gutsy, faith-filled deconstruction will provide all of those in spades.

The temptation scene in Mark's gospel ends by noting that Jesus was with the wild beasts, after which angels attended to him. I love that symbolism: when we wrestle with our faith—with our worldview and our core assumptions—we come face-to-face with some ugly realities, some "wild beasts" that frighten us. But if we stand our ground and endure through the struggle, God is faithful and will console and comfort us. That is the pattern of authentic transformation and growth: first the wild beasts, then the angels.

Deconstructing Dualism

Another reason that deconstruction is so important is that it can help us identify the dualistic themes that have come to be embedded within our worldview. As we deconstruct these concepts and understand them in fresh ways, it becomes increasingly more difficult to live through a dualistic worldview. We see the great truths of Scripture differently, we see the narrative of Scripture differently, and we see ourselves and our calling differently.

I believe there are nine concepts that we are in urgent need of deconstructing, because these concepts tend to trap us in faulty ways of thinking when we fail to clearly understand their true biblical meaning. If we're able to clear away the dualistic baggage attached to them, the result has the power to forever alter our faith. Going "into the desert" to deconstruct and explore these concepts holds the key to reading the Bible for all its worth.

The nine concepts are (in no particular order):

- Sin
- Salvation
- Heaven
- Hell
- The Kingdom of God/Heaven
- Gospel
- Eternal Life
- The World/Worldly
- Flesh

In the following section I will be taking each term and deconstructing it through a biblical, non-dualistic lens. This will enable us to gain a better appreciation for how the deconstructive process can help us critically examine core concepts and deepen our faith.

Sin. Sin is often associated with doing something bad or "below the line" (referring to the dualistic model from the previous chapter), but this is a rather superficial understanding of the biblical concept of sin. Sin is the Bible's word for anything which destroys and distorts God's good creation. Sometimes we associate sin with wrongdoing on a personal level, but sin always affects four dimensions simultaneously: our relationship with ourselves, others, the natural world, and God. Sin always acts like a disease that eats away at the fabric of our lives, eroding our integrity as image-bearers and distorting our ability to reflect the glory of God's love and power into the world. That's why God is so anti-sin. God is fully against that which destroys His valuable creation, and so He can't and won't tolerate sin in any form. To some this seems suffocating or extreme, but because sin is the very thing that *prevents* us from experiencing a full life, how could a good and loving God tolerate it?

One of the most common objections I come across relating to this issues is the following: "If we didn't experience sin, evil, or suffering, we could never fully know and appreciate what was truly good." But this line of thinking implies that sin helps us find meaning and purpose within our world, and that it helps us identify what is true, noble, right, and just. This paradigm is completely unbiblical in its foundation, as it assumes that in God's very good original creation, something was missing (i.e., sin) that was needed to fully appreciate and understand God and the created world's goodness.

The Bible's witness is overwhelmingly clear in its insistence that sin, in whatever form it is expressed, only detracts from experiencing the richness God offers us in this life. That's why, when we welcome sin into our lives or hold a flippant attitude towards sin, we are doing more than offending God—we're actually robbing ourselves from the deeper, more intense pleasures that only come to us as we walk away from sin and embrace God's goodness.

Salvation. While many within the church have heard the word salvation again and again, few can offer a definition when asked for one. Salvation is one of those Christianeze words that is repeated so much and explained so little that very few people know what they're talking about when they use the term.

Salvation simply means *rescue*. Whenever God delivers His people from destruction or peril the Bible declares that God has *saved* (rescued) them. In the most general sense, whenever God removes the threat of death, destruction, or disorder, replacing it with His shalom (justice, blessing, and peace), God's people celebrate the fact that God's salvation (rescue) has come.[12]

It's very easy to read the word salvation dualistically, as many Christians have done, and assume it's shorthand for "accepting Jesus' death on the cross in order to have one's sins forgiven and secure entrance into heaven." But that would be similar to taking the word sin and defining it as "doing something bad." Salvation is a theologically rich term that shouldn't be reduced to something simplistic.

Salvation is a central theme in both the Old and New Testaments. Throughout the Scriptures salvation is understood as both an event and

---

12 e.g., Psalm 13:5; 14:7; 37:39; 69:2; 118:14; 119:74; Luke 19:9; Romans 11:11; 13:11

process. For example, through Christ God has *saved* us from the penalty of sin (e.g., Romans 8:1), but God is also *saving* us from the power of sin (e.g., Philippians 2:12). Being saved from the penalty of sin (i.e., justification) is an event; it is instantaneous and eternally binding. Being saved from the power of sin (i.e., sanctification) is a process; it occurs over time through God's Spirit and our participation. It's very appropriate to say that we are *saved* in Christ and that we are also *being saved* in Christ.

We can also mistakenly assume that the goal of God's salvation is to rescue us *from* this world into heaven. But that assumption betrays the purpose behind the term itself and the broader theme of redemption we find in the Bible. God's salvation is not about being saved *from* this world. God's salvation is about being saved *for* this world (e.g., Ephesians 2:10). God again and again rescues His people from sin and death in order that they may be free—*in this world*—to live for Him and work to liberate those who are under the oppression of sin.

The term salvation in the Old Testament specifically connotes a broadening or enlarging. The Bible's message is that sin binds, constrains, imprisons, and suffocates us. But when God saves us, His salvation moves us into an open, safe space where we are free from harm and can experience freedom, prosperity, and well-being. We are then called to take that freedom, prosperity, and well-being into the world and into our relationships. We are saved—we are *rescued*—so that we can participate with God in the saving of His world.

Heaven. Heaven is perhaps one of the most dualistically laced terms of the nine we are working through. Many think of heaven as a place where God lives, often disconnected and distant from the world in which we live. But again, this has more to do with dualistic assumptions than biblical evidence.

As theologian NT Wright often says, "Heaven is God's space." It is God's unpolluted dimension that overlaps and interlocks with reality as we experience it. Normally hidden from our sight, heaven is occasionally revealed or unveiled so that people can see God's dimension running concurrent with everyday, ordinary life (e.g., 2 Kings 6.17; Revelation 1). That heaven is sometimes understood as *unveiled* is significant to note, because it creates a picture where heaven is closer than we might imagine. Instead of a place "out there," far removed from our lived experience, heaven is "not far from each of us" (Acts 17:27).

Heaven is not the permanent location of God's people after death, as if it were the final destination in God's grand plan. What kind of plan would that be? Is the goal of God's saving efforts to abandon this world and have us live forever somewhere else? In what sense would that complete God's redemptive and restorative work? It doesn't even make sense logically.

The Bible makes it abundantly clear (e.g., Revelation 21 and 22) that God's goal is the redemption of His *entire* creation, and that one day His space (i.e., heaven) will be fully joined and integrated with our space (i.e., earth). Should we be surprised? In Genesis we see that sin expelled Adam and Eve from the garden. *But God was also expelled!* God's passion is to restore the intimate relationship with humanity we He once had when He walked as one of us in His world (Genesis 3:8).

All of this means that heaven is not our home, and it's not God's either. God has always felt comfortable in what we think of as our world. That's why He's so intent on saving and restoring it. He doesn't want us to live in His space forever; He wants to live with us in ours (Revelation 21:3).

Hell. One can't talk about heaven without touching upon its perceived opposite: hell. Our word hell comes from the Hebrew word *Gehenna*, which was a literal place located in the valley of Hinnon on the south-west slope of Jerusalem. In Jesus' day it was used as a garbage dump, and it smouldered with continual fire. At the time some Jews used it as an image for the place of punishment after death. Jesus' own usage, however, does not simply localize hell to a reality *after* physical death, but builds upon the image to warn of the possibility of one's life becoming a living hell through the pervasive, poisoning influence of sin.

In fact, I believe Jesus' primary intent in his usage of the term hell was to teach us what we can expect our lives—*in this world*—to look and feel like if we pursue anti-God (i.e., sinful) ways of living. Jesus' references to hell (e.g. Matt. 5:22, 29; 10:28; 12:33) are not just an apt metaphor for describing God's final judgement against those who reject His offer of rescue; they reveal that our lives can become a "hell on earth" if we fail to turn away from sin and its crippling, destructive power.

The Kingdom of Heaven/God. Every culture has catchphrases that are used to convey larger, more complex meanings. These catchphrases often can't be understood in a different context simply by defining every word literally and piecing them together. For example, if I was watching a football game where one player was dominating, at some point I might say, "He's in the zone!" Someone completely unfamiliar with our culture would have no idea what I was talking about. They might ask, "What zone?" and totally miss what I was trying to communicate.

Most of us know that when someone says, "He's in the zone!" they are referring to a heightened athletic state where composure, athleticism, focus, and intensity all collide to produce an abnormal, superior performance. But we'd never describe such an event with that kind of technical language because it's too wordy and awkward. Instead we create our own cultural catchphrase to convey the same meaning, but more efficiently. Over time everyone comes to understand what we mean when we use the catchphrase.

It's the same with Jesus' phrase "the kingdom of heaven/God."[13] We can't just define each word and then put them together, because we'll miss what was embedded into this 1st century expression. The kingdom of heaven/God is not a *place* (i.e., heaven), but a *state* we can enter into during this life. "Entering the kingdom of heaven" (Matthew 21:32) does not mean "going to heaven after death," but is instead referring to what we'll experience if we allow God's rule as King to occur throughout our lives. In the 1st century Jews used this phrase to describe the experience of living under the rule and reign of God in everyday life. To live within the kingdom of heaven/God was to live a life inside of God's rule and

---

13 Matthew's gospel frequently uses the term "kingdom of heaven" while Mark and Luke always use "kingdom of God." The use of the word "heaven" in these instances is a way of referring to God without using His name, which Jews and Jewish Christians believed to be too holy to pronounce or even write.

power, both personally and socially. Individually speaking, entering the kingdom of God meant recalibrating one's attitudes and actions towards the worship and love of God. Socially, Jews talked about the kingdom of God "breaking forth" wherever God's will was being done "on earth as in heaven," that is, wherever God's power and presence invaded and transformed broken realities like poverty, oppression, idolatry, etc.

Dualistically understood, Jesus' teachings on the kingdom of heaven/God are almost always assumed to be teachings on *how to get to heaven*. But none of Jesus' parables on the kingdom make sense if the term is understood as a heavenly destination. However, if we substitute "the power and presence of God" or "God's rule in your life" when we read "the kingdom of heaven/God," Jesus' teachings take on new and profound relevance for *this* life.

Gospel. The word gospel literally means *good news*, and it's another loaded term that was used and understood very differently in Jesus' day than it is today. Unfortunately, "believing in the gospel" has come to be understood as a synonym for the term salvation. The gospel, in this understanding, is the good news that because of Jesus' sacrificial death on the cross, our sins can be forgiven and we are assured of life in heaven forever. But like salvation, the term gospel meant something very different to Jesus and the early church.

For Jews living during the time of Jesus, the word gospel had its roots in the prophetic book of Isaiah, and meant the news of God's long-awaited victory over evil and the rescue (i.e., salvation) of His people.

For Gentiles (non-Jews) living within the Roman world the gospel was the "good news" that Caesar—the head of the world's most powerful empire—was the true king and ruler of the world.

When the New Testament writers (especially Paul) connected the word gospel to Jesus, both the assumptions of Jewish listeners and Gentile listeners were overturned. To the Jew, Paul was claiming that in Jesus this long-awaited victory over evil and the salvation of God's people had been achieved. To the Gentile, Paul declared again and again (often at the start of each of his letters) that the Lord and Saviour of the world was not Caesar, but Jesus!

The gospel announcement is that through Jesus God offers full salvation and deliverance from evil. That's because Jesus is now above every earthly power (even those within our modern world), and you and I are free to live under Jesus, a King who's willing to die for us so that we can flourish and "take hold of the life that is truly life" (1 Timothy 6:19). To embrace this gospel is to embrace the fact that Jesus is Lord over all. He is the rightful ruler of the world, and the rightful ruler of our lives. This gospel does not give us hope for the *next* life alone; it gives us hope for *this* life. As that understanding takes hold of us, it begins to reshape our lives as we live under Jesus' authority and power.

Eternal Life. The concept of "eternal life" does not mean "existence continuing without end," but we could innocently assume this if we just put the literal definition of both words together. When I discussed the meaning behind the phrase "the kingdom of heaven" I used the sports analogy of an athlete being "in the zone" as an example of a cultural catchphrase. But that metaphor also becomes a very helpful one when talking about the concept of eternal life. Eternal life is a shorthand way of getting at the idea of "life lived in all its fullness" or "the kind of life God intends." When people came to Jesus and asked about eternal life, they weren't asking how to live forever or gain entrance into heaven. They were asking, "How do I find 'the zone' or 'sweet spot' in this life? How do I take hold of life in all its fullness?" Jesus' response to them was that when we live life within the power and presence of God (i.e., when we enter the kingdom of heaven), we will find ourselves experiencing "eternal life"—life "in the zone." We will find that we're taking hold of the kind of life God desires for us. Ironically, Jesus' teachings on eternal life have less to do with eternity and more to do with our lives in the here and now.

The World/Worldly. When we come to the New Testament wearing dualistic lenses, there are a lot of stumbling blocks we'll encounter. One of the most significant is the concept of "the world" (or "worldly"). Dualistically, "the world" is assumed to mean the earth and all that is in it, and it's also often assumed to be the antithesis of heaven. But both of these assumptions are incorrect.

It's very important to note that when the authors of the New Testament use either of these terms[14] they are actually using a catchphrase that means "ways of living that express themselves in anti-God, anti-Christ, and anti-life ways." Being "worldly" has nothing to do with whether someone is cultured, educated, or even invested in material reality. It is not a subtly

14 e.g., 1 Corinthians 3:3; 2 Corinthians 1:12; 2 Corinthians 1:17; Titus 2:12; James 4:4.

dualistic encouragement to avoid this earthly, material dimension and instead pursue the eternal, heavenly one. The Bible's condemnation of "the world" and "worldliness" is not a condemnation of creation generally or the earth specifically. Worldliness is a way of describing ways of living within God's creation that bring death and destruction upon ourselves, each other, the natural world, and our relationship with God. To stand against "the world" shouldn't be understood to mean "stand against God's creation." Biblically we are called to serve, steward, and bring out the potential within created reality.[15] However, we are to divorce ourselves from worldly (i.e., anti-God) behaviours and attitudes because they prevent us from entering the kingdom of heaven/God (i.e., God's power and presence in everyday life).

Flesh. The tension between God's Spirit and "the flesh" that the New Testament speaks to[16] is often misinterpreted as a struggle between God's Spirit and our physical bodies. But that is not what the Bible is trying to convey. The use of "flesh" in the New Testament is not a synonym for body or in any way meant to reinforce a dualistic view of the body's inferiority.

One's mind is just as polluted by sin as one's body, so the answer is not to reject one or the other. Both are gifts from God! "The flesh" is a shorthand way of referring to the sinful impulses that are alive and well in all of us. Notice that I said *sinful* impulses, because not all impulses are sinful. Impulses that are directed towards God are powerful forces

---

15 Genesis 1:28.
16 John 3:6; John 6:63; 1 Corinthians 15:50; Philippians 3:3.

for good and transformation. But impulses that are directed away from God do nothing but end in death (Romans 3:23).

The conflict between the flesh and the Spirit is not between one part of us and another part of us but rather between us and the Holy Spirit of God. "The flesh" refers to our sinful disposition to pursue self-centred ends through self-sufficient means. It refers to the posture of trying to live out lives independently from God as if we didn't need Him.

Paul identifies "sexual immorality, impurity, depravity, idolatry, sorcery, hostilities, strife, jealousy, outbursts of anger, selfish rivalries, dissensions, factions, envying, murder, drunkenness, carousing, and similar things" (Galatians 5:19-21) as manifestations of the flesh—the anti-God impulses that rise up through the following self-serving desires:

1. The desire for control and power.
2. The desire for self-gratification.

When the New Testament warns us concerning the sins of the flesh, it is warning us against allowing these motivations and impulses to take control in our lives.

Wrestling with God

What would happen if we could really *get* the biblical meaning behind these concepts? What would we discover the next time we read through our favourite book of the Bible? How would our understanding of discipleship change if we read through the gospels with these terms freshly deconstructed?

The concepts I've outlined above are critical for us to wrestle with. They are "gateway concepts," meaning that how we understand them will colour our entire understanding of the Bible and its message. That's why they are worth the time and energy deconstruction demands. But we need to remember that deconstruction does not offer quick-fix solutions or easy answers. It is a challenging journey and process, but one that will make our faith real and grounded.

In the book of Genesis, Jacob (like Jesus) finds himself in the desert. Jacob encounters God and wrestles with Him throughout the night. Jacob overcomes his opponent and receives a blessing from God. But amidst the struggle Jacob finds that he has been injured, and from that day forward forever walks with a limp as a reminder of his encounter with God.

Deconstruction invites us into a similar encounter. It invites us to leave the clichés and pat answers behind, and journey into unfamiliar places where we will feel alone and afraid. But we will encounter God in these "deserts," and if we struggle—if we wrestle and overcome—our walk of faith will never be the same. The rewards from our struggle will prove to be rich. But remember: first the wild beasts, then the angels.

PART II money, sex, and power

4 a good eye

Why spend money on what is not bread,
and your labour on what does not satisfy?

~ Isaiah 55:1-2

When I was a child I was diagnosed with a genetic disorder related to my eyes. I was told that without having a corneal transplant surgery I would become legally blind by the time I was ten years old. Thankfully, at the age of nine I had my first corneal transplant, a procedure where the diseased part of my eye (in this case my cornea) was removed and replaced by a donor's cornea. Many corneal transplants have followed since that time, but not all of them have been successful. In fact, as I write these pages my left eye has no vision at all due to complications from a tissue rejection, while my right eye is clear and healthy. I literally have one good eye and one bad eye.

Having a good eye and bad eye were two 1st century expressions that were commonly known by all Jews. When describing someone who was generous, people would comment that the person had a *good eye*. Conversely, if someone was thought to be selfish and tight-fisted, they were described as having a *bad eye*. It seems that these expressions were an attempt to highlight the Jewish idea that what one does with their resources reveals a lot about their spiritual health.

In Jesus' day, to have a *good eye* inferred that one saw the world clearly. With a *good eye* one could perceive God's intentions for us as humans and discern His ancient call to reflect His image through graciousness, goodness, and generosity. Someone with such an outlook was one who lived out of a deep awareness that God's blessing and favour was never meant to be hoarded, but to be shared in joy with others. This idea was formative for Jesus, who incorporated it into his teachings:

> "The eye is the lamp of the body. If your eyes are good, your whole body will be full of light. But if your eyes are bad, your whole body will be full of darkness. If then the light within you is darkness, how great is that darkness!" (Matthew 6:22-23)

When Jesus said, "if your eyes are bad, your whole body will be full of darkness" he meant that if we fail to be generous with what we have, we'll cut ourselves off from God's luminous goodness (i.e., "light") and our lives will become cold, dark, and empty.

Those are strong words, but would anyone disagree? Have you ever met people with a bad eye? People who are completely self-absorbed and stingy with what God has given them? They aren't the most inspiring or likeable people. You can only spend so much time around them before you begin to feel the negativity and shallowness that comes with such an outlook on life.

Now contrast that with people you know that possesses a good eye. They are generous with their time, energy, and money. They have an infectious, positive energy that causes them to radiate an uncommon warmth and joy into the lives of those around them. Because of this people are drawn to them and long to be more like them.

Jesus calls us to become people with a good eye, and the older I get the more exciting this invitation becomes. I want God to teach me to see properly, live generously, and grow into a disciple who lives out of an open-handed spirit that loves, shares, and gives in ways that are "full of light."

One of the realities I have to face with my physical eye condition is that I can't control whether I can see rightly. Something may happen that could lead to my eventual blindness (I can only have so many corneal transplants before they will cease to be effective), and one day I may find myself with two bad eyes, unable to do anything about it. Circumstances beyond my control may render my world dark. But as a disciple I can *choose* to develop a good eye. I can choose—starting today—to hone my spiritual vision so that I begin to live a life characterised by inappropriate generosity towards others.

The Conversion of the Wallet

Martin Luther once remarked that there are two conversions: the first is of the heart, the second is of the wallet. It's so true. It is so much easier to give God something nebulous like "my life" than give Him the resources that I touch, hold, and rely on every day. For most people the movement towards becoming more generous begins with a commitment to give more time and energy in the service of others. This is a noble decision, but Jesus' plan to help us develop a good eye starts in a different place. Notice the verses that immediately precede his teachings on having a good eye:

> *"Do not store up for yourselves treasures on earth, where moth and rust destroy, and where thieves break in and steal. But store up for yourselves treasures in heaven, where moth and rust do not destroy, and where thieves do not break in and steal. For where your treasure is, there your heart will be also."* (Matthew 6:19-21)

When Jesus is talking about storing up treasure he isn't talking about volunteer hours. He's talking about the *literal* treasures we want to protect. He's talking about our wealth and our stuff. For Jesus the starting point of cultivating a good eye is changing how we use our financial resources (whether those are large or meagre). More specifically,

Jesus wants us to re-examine where we *invest* our money. His counsel is unavoidably simple and direct, and we need to take it seriously as disciples. If I had to paraphrase Matthew 6:19-21, it might read like this:

> *"Whatever you invest in always, over time, becomes the thing you love most. Our attention and heart follow what we invest in. Therefore, does it make any sense to invest in stuff that can be stolen or is here today and gone tomorrow? Instead, invest in the only two things that ultimately matter: God and His kingdom. When you do, you'll find your heart following, and you'll develop a good eye."*

To most people Jesus' teachings seem backwards. I've heard people say that Christians/churches don't need to push monetary giving because as people grow spiritually they'll just *want* to give more. Jesus, however, doesn't assume that this is the way reality works. According to him, *first* we give and *then* the feelings and desires to give will come, not vice versa. "For where your treasure is [invested], there your heart *will be* also." In other words, the *current location of our treasure (monetary investment) is the eventual location of our heart (our passion and desire)*. If we wait until we *feel* like being generous with our money, we'll probably be waiting a long time. In my experience, we're all very good at evading the demands of generosity by rationalizing our responsibilities away.

"I give in *other* ways."

"I can't afford to give."

"I don't feel called to give."

"I'm still praying and thinking about it."

Let me be very honest and admit that I rarely *feel* like giving away my money. Giving is a spiritual discipline that I practice, not because it feels good or is easy, but because I want to be a disciple with a good eye who is becoming more like Jesus. And believe me, whoever came up with the term spiritual *discipline* was right. It isn't super-fun-happy-time, and it's doesn't come easily or naturally. However, it is absolutely critical to a rich life.

I think deep down we all want to experience a rich, fulfilling life. I also think that in our best moments we all want to be generous people. And I think most of us understand, at least intuitively, the connection between these desires. But my experience has taught me that if we don't put a plan in place regarding how we are going to become more generous with our resources, then months and years will go by and our good intentions will go for naught. At some point every disciple needs to develop a *strategy* on how they are going to invest their God-given treasures and start developing a good eye.

The bad news is we won't find a lot of people offering help or guidance. In our society, about the only thing we teach related to money is how to *spend* it[17]. In fact there aren't many places (including churches) where we can get help on how to use money in wise, helpful, God-

17 One exception to this is that our society *will* get serious about teaching people how to use money once they are in financial ruin (i.e. bankruptcy). Think about that: our society is committed to teaching people how to use money *after they ruin their lives through mismanaging it!*

honouring ways. Even if our churches *do* offer financial coaching, these services are almost always aimed at adults with "real" jobs. Very few people are teaching emerging leaders how to develop a good eye through their use of money. How much sense does that make? Most people start working around fifteen or so (babysitting, a part-time job, etc.) and even though they may not be making a ton of money, they are still making money. With every pay check that comes in they are developing habits around spending, saving, and giving. If no one is helping to shape those early spending, saving, and giving habits in healthy and wise ways, then most of us will default to using our money like we see others around us using it (and there aren't many role models in our society or in our churches when it comes to handling money wisely). If we just do what we see everyone else doing, it's like the blind leading the blind and we all end up paying a heavy price; we end up plunging into a pit of financial ruin together.

Financing Fulfillment

The famous novelist Jane Austen once wrote: "A large income is the best recipe for happiness I have ever heard of." Do you believe that? I want to disagree, but…if someone asked me how much money I needed to be happy, I'd probably say, "Just a little bit more." We're so good at fooling ourselves, aren't we? We say one thing and then totally contradict ourselves in the next breathe. For instance, a Princeton study found that 89 percent of people believed our society is "too materialistic." I guess they meant *other* people, because 84 percent in the *same survey* said it was "very or fairly important" to have "a beautiful home, a new car, and other nice things."

I believe that one of the most destructive ideas that exists today is that our fulfillment can be financed; that the surest route to happiness is a higher income and more stuff. Our culture is in the midst of an outbreak of *affluenza*[18] and we all need a vaccine that will protect us from its life-crippling effects.

The vaccine that God has offered us is the way of Jesus, which is a lifestyle practice that teaches us to see that meaning doesn't come through money. We may not think of Jesus as an expert on money, but his advice on the subject is pure gold. Quite a few of Jesus' teachings deal directly or indirectly with money, and I respect him a lot for that. Talking about money isn't easy in any culture, but Jesus had the courage to confront our preferred sicknesses and offer us a way to find healing and health. In characteristic fashion Jesus cut to the chase on this issue during his sermon on the mount:

> *"No one can serve two masters. Either he will hate the one and love the other, or he will be devoted to the one and despise the other. You cannot serve both God and Money."*
> (Matthew 6:24)

Jesus' message is clear. If we intend to follow him as disciples and find healing from the affluenza that blinds us to life's goodness and

---

18 A contagion that poisons us with the idea that the things that matter most in life have a price tag attached to them.

beauty, it will mean a radical commitment to drastically change how we understand and use our money. That change begins as we confront some hard truths about money.

Money is not *evil*, but it is *powerful*. For too long 1 Timothy 6:9-10 has been misquoted, and often by people holding to a dualistic view which sees money as worldly and inherently bad/sinful:

> *"People who want to get rich fall into temptation and a trap and into many foolish and harmful desires that plunge men into ruin and destruction. For the love of money is a root of all kinds of evil. Some people, eager for money, have wandered from the faith and pierced themselves with many griefs."* (1 Timothy 6:9-10)

It's not *money*, but the *love of money* that is the problem. Money isn't evil, but money *is* powerful. Therefore we need to be very careful how we *direct* it (e.g., selfish/sinful ways vs. godly/wise ways), since *that* decision will make the difference between developing a good eye or a bad eye.

The metaphor I always use here is that of an explosion. The force from an explosion is powerful, and if it's directed properly (e.g. combustion in a car's engine) then it can be a source of blessing in our lives. However, if Youtube has taught us anything, it's that an undirected explosion can cause irrevocable damage to ourselves and others (albeit with some hilarious results!).

Money is a resource for building God's kingdom. Money isn't an end in itself; it's a means to a greater end. That greater end is the kingdom of God, and as disciples we should be passionate about giving to the kingdom work we see unfolding around us. When we see money as an end in itself, or a means to achieving our own ends or agendas, we should expect our world to become filled with the darkness Jesus warned his listeners about.

We are accountable to God for how faithfully we steward what He's entrusted to us. Strictly speaking, the money we have isn't ours, we're just *stewarding* it on God's behalf. A steward is someone who is placed in charge of something valuable and expected to care for and use it wisely. Everything we have comes from God (James 1:17). If we're tempted to think that it's our talent, skill, or superior intelligence that has lead to the prosperity we enjoy, God warns us to, "remember the Lord your God, for it is He who gives you the ability to produce wealth" (Deuteronomy 8:17-18).

Do we take this stewardship responsibility seriously? Do we assume that because the money is in *our* bank accounts, we're not accountable to anyone but ourselves? Jesus' parable of the talents in Matthew 25:14-30 clearly teaches that God rewards those who faithfully steward what God has entrusted to them. But it also clearly teaches that God will eventually stop investing His wealth in those who are unfaithful in their stewardship responsibilities.

We are to put our hope in God, not money. To an emerging leader named Timothy the apostle Paul once wrote the following:

"Command those who are rich in this present world not to be arrogant nor to put their hope in wealth, which is so uncertain, but to put their hope in God, who richly provides us with everything for our enjoyment." (1 Timothy 6:17)

Ok, sounds great. But how do we know we're putting our hope in God and not money? A friend once told me he knows when he's in a place where he's trusting in God and not his money when he can give his money away. I think he's right. We tend to cling desperately to the things we are staking our lives on. Our ability to let go of our money is one of the clearest indications that we don't look to it as our Lord and Saviour.

We should enjoy the material blessings money can provide, but we must extend those blessings to others. Jesus once told a parable about a rich fool in Luke 12:13-21. In the parable a man's field produced a huge crop and so he decided to build a bigger storehouse so that he could retire from his work and, "Take life easy; eat drink and be merry" (verse 19). However, that very night God took the man's life. Why? Well, one might think that the problem was the man's intent to set up a life of ease and merriment. But I think the deeper problem lay in the fact that the man was only looking to make *his* life easier and merrier. He hoarded his money instead of sharing it with his community. He didn't even consider extending the benefits of his wealth to others, and was fixated on how he alone could benefit from his riches. The point Jesus was making through this story is that if we find ourselves in a season of life where we're experiencing a "huge crop," we need to remember that God always blesses us so that we can extend those blessings to others.

A Plan for Financial Fitness

Let's get practical. It's one thing to talk through a theology of money, but unless we connect that to our day-to-day habits we won't get very far. Let's work on a strategy so that we can begin to cultivate a good eye.

There are only three things we can do with money: spend it, save it, or give it away. A disciple needs to focus on all three of those activities, and put a plan in place for how to *spend wisely, save prudently,* and *give generously*. For the reflections that follow, I'll be offering two tracks. The first is for those with no fixed expenses (i.e., you aren't paying for rent, food, etc.). The second will be for those *with* fixed expenses.

Spend Wisely. When I talk about spending money, I'm referring to how we spend the money we have on *ourselves*. How does being a disciple affect these spending decisions? In every possible way! However, for the purpose of simplifying things, I think two principles should frame our spending habits, and those are simplicity and restraint.

I really believe that a disciple should be moving towards simplicity in all areas of their life. This is especially true for their finances and how much they spend on themselves. Simplicity involves focusing on spending money on our *needs* and reducing our spending on frivolous *wants*. Living simply is another spiritual discipline that aims to reduce the clutter in our lives. Sometimes the clutter is the result of *doing* too many things, and sometimes the clutter is the result of *having* too many

liberty to direct those funds to other organizations, charities or causes as you see fit, but that first 10% belongs to your home church.

Second Sight

When I talk with emerging leaders about these three habits, giving is the one that is the hardest pill for them to swallow. I think it's because if we are truly giving money away, we will likely never experience a direct benefit from it. I may spend less money, but at least I'm still spending it on *myself*. I may save more money, but at least I'm saving it for future opportunities that interest *me*. With spending plans and saving plans, we're figuring out how to gain financially for *our own benefit*. When we put together giving plans, we're figuring out how to *lose* financially *for the benefit of others*.

It's never exciting to lose. But the paradox of Jesus' message is that sometimes we win by losing. Even Jesus "was rich, yet for your sakes he became poor, so that you through his poverty might become rich" (2 Corinthians 8:9). I know that whether we commit to giving away 10% or 20% of our income, it's unlikely we'll find this decision exciting. But we need to remember that for Jesus having a good eye *starts* with giving our money away and investing it in others.

So if you have no fixed expenses the breakdown is 50/30/20 in terms of spending, saving, and giving. If you find yourself paying for rent, food, utilities, etc. your spending portion will be necessarily bigger, but I would still set a goal to move towards an 80/10/10 lifestyle. For either situation that might not be possible overnight, but you can do something starting tomorrow if you're serious about cultivating a good eye. Spend a little less. Set up a savings account. Commit to give regularly to your church.

Now you might be defensive at this point and want to disagree with some or all of what I've outlined above. You're free to do so. I guess it comes down to how deeply you want to embed Jesus' teachings into your life. I can't make you want to be a disciple who has a good eye. All I can do is offer you what I think is a good way to get there.

We cannot call ourselves disciples and ignore the issue of how we use the resources God has entrusted to us. The blessings and curses attached to wise or unwise uses of money are too significant and too much is at stake. That's why Jesus isn't silent on the subject. He has a passion to help us use what we've been given in ways that lead to genuine fulfillment and joy. Much of the time, that will mean redirecting our wealth away from our own profit.

I hope you learn much earlier than I did that you can't find meaning through money, and that you can't finance fulfillment. In a world stricken with affluenza, a world blind in its pursuit of "just a little more," may you pursue a good eye and find through your generosity that it is indeed "more blessed to give than to receive" (Acts 20:35).

5 the beautiful risk

*I have often wondered why God would give his creatures such a
strong and constant fascination with one another's image, form, and face.
Why would God take such a risk unless it were an important risk?
What is the connection between our human passion and knowing God?
Are all relationships a school of communion?
These are the truly religious questions that we must dare to ask.*

~ Richard Rohr

Sex is a beautiful risk. *Beautiful* because when we humans get sex right, there isn't much that can compete with this rapturous, good, amazing gift from God. *Risk* because when we get it wrong, there isn't much that can compete with the confusion, heartache, and dehumanization that results. In ways that are not easy to explain, humans are shaped in profound ways by sex. Understanding why is only possible if we explore how sex is intimately connected to the larger contexts of love, relationships, and what it means to be human.

In the first chapter of Genesis we read that God created everything and created everything "very good" (Genesis 1:31). Soon afterwards, however, we read about the first "not good" within the creation story. After creating Adam, God declared that it was "not good for man to be alone" (Genesis 2:18). Up to this point the only descriptor God had used for His creation had been "very good." Notice that the first "not good" within creation was a statement regarding human community and relationship. Specifically, that Adam would not flourish and develop as intended as long as he remained alone. Adam needed community in order to be fully alive to himself, the world, and God.

God declared Adam's isolation to be "not good," not simply because it's not God's design for humans, but because it's not His design for *anything* within creation. Relationships are the foundation of reality. Our world is one which is built upon and sustained by a myriad of networks and connections—seen and unseen. This foundation stems from the fact that God *Himself* is a relationship; a mysterious, loving community of Father, Son, and Holy Spirit.[19] Therefore, is it surprising that we as God's image-bearers experience such a deep hunger for love, relationship, and community? To be human is to be created by Love for love; created by Relationship for relationship; created by Community for community.

The declaration that it is not good for us to be alone is something most of us recognize on an instinctual level. Deep within us there is an

---

19 e.g., Matthew 3:16-17; 28:19; 1 Corinthians 12:3-6; 2 Corinthians 13:14

undeniable impulse that drives us from isolation towards connectedness with others. There is nothing worse than feeling isolated, alone, and cut off from others. Conversely, there is nothing better than feeling like there is a community of people who understand you, value you, embrace you, and are willing to share their lives with you.

When God declared that it wasn't good for Adam to be alone, He was condemning more that just the absence of generic community within Adam's life. Adam lacked a helpmate, someone crafted to compliment him and vice versa. Adam needed a kindred spirit and soul mate through which to forge a connection that was even richer than those offered by friendship. It wasn't good for Adam to be without someone he could fall in love with and be completely "naked" (i.e., vulnerable) with.

Once we become aware of our God-given drive towards community, and more specifically our drive to find one with whom we can be "naked and not ashamed" (Genesis 2:25), we begin to understand the power of our sexual drives. Our sexual longings are the physical expression of our God-given impulse to be connected and in right relationship with both Creator and creation. Sex should expand and enhance our knowledge of self and God, as well as draw us into a way of seeing creation as enchanting and wondrous.

But for many of us, instead of enhancing one's journey in a powerful way, sex is the very thing that constricts and inhibits us from accessing life in all its depth and beauty. Some of us have jumped into sex because we believed it was the very thing that would bring us life. We soon learnt that that unless our sexual activity is aligned with God's intentions and design, it will satisfy little except an immediate physical craving.

When we seek out sex before we seek out God our experience will always be disappointing, shallow, and unsatisfying. Sex will never fill the void we want or expect it to. That's because sex is not the answer; sex is the question. It's more obvious to me the older I get that sex was not designed to solve the loneliness that plagues us but to draw us towards the Mystery that can heal us. When we seek first the kingdom of God and allow God to deal with our emotional emptiness and isolation, sex becomes catalytic and enhances every dimension of our lives. When we seek first the kingdom of Self and look to sex to deliver us from the evil of isolation, we find ourselves chasing shadows of unfulfilled expectations.

One of the hardest things to wrap your head around when it comes to any of Scripture's directives is that they aren't arbitrary. Scripture doesn't say what it does because it has to or because it's simply a collection of right answers for moral living. Scripture teaches what it does so that we can know the truth about who God is, who we are, and how to live in a way that maximizes our experience of beauty, goodness, joy, peace, creativity, and adventure. Scripture constantly invites us to see things *the way they really are.*

That perspective on Scripture is essential to remember in the context of sex. It's so easy to create a caricature of God that views Him as a sexually repressed, narrow-minded father figure who delights in telling us how to live because He's on some cosmic power trip. Nothing within the Bible—and especially the life of Jesus—gives us permission to hold such a view. Instead we discover that throughout the course of the entire biblical story God reveals His desire to extravagantly love us and shower us with goodness and grace. Therefore, God's counsel on sex should never be understood as anything other than that which stems from His desire to:

1. Reveal the way things really are so our illusions and excuses don't overtake and destroy us.
2. Set us up to experience a level of sexual fulfillment that few of us would even dare to hope for.

With these two overriding principles in mind, we begin to recognize that God's do's and don'ts (and there are a lot of do's and don'ts when it comes to sex in the Bible[20]) help create the container through which we can experience our sexuality in a way that builds our personal integrity (i.e., personal *integratedness* as human beings) and enhances our lives.

A Case Study: The Church in Corinth

Whether you're married or single, one of the sections of Scripture you'd do well to study and reflect on again and again is 1 Corinthians 6:12-7:9. This section of the Bible is extremely instructive for disciples wrestling through the question of how to cultivate a healthy sexuality that leads to wholeness, fulfillment, and freedom. Over the next few pages I'm going to be walking through this passage, so if you have a Bible nearby, you might find it helpful to track along with me.

---

20 Leviticus 18:6-16; 18:23; Deuteronomy 7:21; 22:25-27; Romans 1:24-27; 1 Corinthians 6:9; 2 Corinthians 12:21; Colossians 3:5; 1 Peter 4:3; 1 Thessalonians 4:3.

1 Corinthians is Paul's first letter to the church in Corinth. Corinth was the Las Vegas of its day. If you could imagine it, you could do it. The city of Corinth was a hypersexual environment where sexual experimentation was welcomed and encouraged. The dominant pagan religions of Corinth incorporated sexual orgies into their worship services as a means to honour the gods and/or provoke them into action. It's fascinating to reflect on the fact that even within this setting, the message and hope of Jesus had begun transforming lives. In an environment that made all forms of sexual pleasure accessible and permissible, the people of Corinth were anything but satisfied and whole. When they heard the gospel many responded and became disciples of Jesus, learning to turn away from the sexual activities that had promised liberation and freedom, but delivered degradation and emptiness.

When those in Corinth turned to Jesus they would have been taught immediately about their need to turn away from the sexual sins they were involved in. But what were they supposed to be turning towards? What were they as disciples supposed to be doing with their sexual urges? Was the answer to abandon sex altogether as something evil and corrupt because of its association with pagan worship? To a church asking these questions Paul responds with 1 Corinthians 6:12-7:9.

Paul starts his teaching by quoting an expression that had been making the rounds in Corinth: "Everything is permissible for me" (verse 12). People apparently thought that if they sinned and just asked God to forgive them through Jesus, then they could do whatever they wanted. Sound familiar? I remember going through that same phase. I felt as if I'd figured out a loophole and had somehow outmanoeuvred God. Through a "get dirty, rinse, and repeat" cycle I could sin, confess and move on as if nothing had happened and there were no consequences to face.

But God through Paul's writing wanted the Corinthian church (and us) to realize something critical to discipleship: we never get the most out of this life by engaging in acts that are sinful, because sinful actions by their very nature obscure and demean our humanness. *God never tries to prevent us from anything that enriches our lives.* It's exactly the opposite. Yes, the pleasures of sin have their season (Hebrews 11:25), but the end result is always death. That death can be physical, emotional, relational, and/or spiritual, but sin never delivers anything good into our lives.

That's why Paul wrote, "'Everything is permissible for me'—but not everything is beneficial." Paul was coaching them towards maturity as disciples. The Corinthian Christians (like us today) needed to learn that maturity begins to take root when we give up what we *could* do for what we *should* do; when we reject what *feels* right and embrace what God *declares* to be right.

When I was a teenager one of the questions my friends and I always wrestled with was, "When it comes to the physical dimension within dating relationships, how far is too far?" We knew the Bible spoke out against sexual immorality, and specifically called for sex to be reserved for the marriage bed (or the marriage car, the marriage kitchen floor, etc.), but at what point did *physical* affection become *sexual* affection? Looking back I think we were well meaning, but we were also misdirected in our questioning. As disciples we shouldn't have been focusing on how much we could get away with in a relationship. Instead, we should have been asking, "What do we need to be doing in order to nurture a healthy sexuality that honours God?"

"How much can I get away with?" is such an immature and self-serving question, and as disciples we need to move away from self-centred thinking. "What should I be doing to nurture a healthy sexuality that honours God?" has a bigger picture in mind than simply getting what *I* want. It leads us into larger, selfless questions that extend to the needs and requirements of both God and others. Once we shift our thinking from the former to the latter, we are ready to hear the rest of God's instruction when it comes to sex and sexuality.

In verse 13 Paul writes: "The body is not meant for sexual immorality, but for the Lord, and the Lord for the body." Did you pick up on the non-dualistic language? Jesus isn't the Lord of my *mind* or *spirit*, but my *body* as well. That means that my body (and by implication my sexuality) is designed to bring glory and delight to God. This is very important to own in the core of our being, because again we are being confronted with the biblical assertion that God is not trying to keep us from experiencing the full pleasures linked to our bodies and sex. He is trying to teach us how to experience these pleasures in their fullness. This means, however, that if He's good at all He'll warn us against any misdirected uses of sex.

God's directives are there to keep us from destructive ends and ensure that when the time is right, we'll be ready for sex as He intended it to be experienced. If we miss that, and if we get caught in an immature way of seeing all limits as oppressive and restrictive, then we'll miss the point of Paul's entire discourse on sexual ethics (and much of discipleship by the way!). To dismiss boundaries as obsolete and outdated is to embrace a life full of heartache and alienation—exactly what we're trying to avoid. It's not until we see boundaries as the context for blessing (in every area of life, not just sex) that the weight of God's wisdom will begin to press upon us. When it does, our desire to live within His parameters will fortify.

In verses 19-20 Paul writes:

> "Do you not know that your body is a temple of the Holy Spirit, who is in you, whom you have received from God? You are not your own; you were bought at a price. Therefore honor God with your body." (1 Corinthians 6:19-20)

God's Spirit lives within us as a disciples of Jesus, so our bodies (and therefore our sexuality) is a *gift* and not an *entitlement*. Our culture says it's a *right*, but that's an incredibly short-sighted, immature and anti-Christian perspective. Our sexuality isn't a resource we get to exploit for our own benefit but something we have a God-given calling to steward wisely. Stewardship may be a word we only associate with money, but everything—including our sexuality—is a gift from God, given to use with specific rights and responsibilities. Therefore, we have to think carefully and consistently about what it means to *steward our sexuality* in ways that glorify God and move us towards a full and pleasurable experience of life.

Learning to Sexually Bless Others

A healthy sex life is something that enhances life and our experience and understanding of God. But God is consistently clear that He's crafted humans in such a way that we can only find that ultimate, rich expression within a married context where two people are passionately committed to pleasuring each other. Within such a relationship God's desires for our sexuality can be fulfilled as each person focuses on sexually blessing the other through creativity and selflessness.

Who doesn't want that? Obviously we all do, it's just that most of us want that experience *right now*.[21] We want God to deliver that kind of sexual fulfillment into our lives now as singles and later within our marriage. At the very least, we'd like to steal away bits and pieces of that experience while we're single.

Listen, I'm not naïve. I remember what it was like to be a young, single, red-blooded disciple who burned with passion (1 Corinthians 7:9). Whether you're in a relationship or not, it can seem impossible at times to resist the impulses that are pulling you towards sex. That's why the best advice you can put into practice, as someone who is single, is to busy yourself with *sexually blessing others*. Does that sound contradictory? It isn't. A disciple's goal should be to sexually bless everyone in their life—

---

21 Remember our reflections on the nature of Satan's temptations in chapter 3?

whether they are married or not. It's just that what it means to sexually bless someone looks different on the unmarried side of the marriage commitment.

Within marriage the way you sexually bless your lover is to selflessly engage in any sexual play that is fulfilling and pleasurable to the other. *Outside* of marriage the way you sexually bless someone is to selflessly *restrain* yourself from sexual play and protect them[22] from faltering in the sexual arena. We normally don't think of celibacy and restraint as *expressions* of our sexuality, but that is exactly what they are. They are expressions of our commitment to nurture habits that protect ourselves and others from sexual heartache and pain. If we don't learn the disciplines of restraint and self-control before marriage we're in for a rude awakening once we put on a wedding ring. That's because a wedding ring doesn't change who you are. Marriage isn't some spiritual switch that causes internal patterns to turn on or shut off. If you are lustful and impulsive before your marriage ceremony you'll be that way the first day of your honeymoon. If you haven't learned to say no to yourself and your physical urges before marriage, it doesn't become easier afterwards. *Pre-marital disciplines are critical because of post-marital realities.* Those who really understand this find it easier to understand and appreciate why God has to train us during seasons of singleness to not give in to what is physically easy and convenient.

---

22 Later in this same letter to the Corinthians church Paul will go on to note that genuine love for someone protects (1 Corinthians 13:7), and that means that in any relationship that could become sexual, we must do everything we can to protect the integrity, sexual purity, and reputations involved.

It's within the context of sexual temptation and restraint that I think it's important to bring up masturbation. I'm not convinced that in and of itself masturbation is always sinful. However, if we default to it too often and without much resistance, we are literally training ourselves in a self-centred way of receiving pleasure. This doesn't actually build into us the habits that will help us enter into a fulfilling sexual relationship once married. I'll have more to say about masturbation and its place within a God-glorifying sexuality below.

A Guide to Pre-Marital Sexuality

When we're single, what most of us probably need is a guide to pre-marital sexuality; a guide that connects our present difficulties with God's future vision of an incredible sexual relationship within marriage. The tensions we face as unmarried sexual creatures are immense. When marriage feels like a lifetime away, dealing with our sexual drives and impulses can feel like we're fighting a losing battle. That's why I want to suggest some concrete ways that you can realistically deal with the sexual pressures that you feel.

First, let me start by saying that I strongly believe that our sexual urges and longings should not *automatically* be categorized as lust. Sometimes (often?) these desires are simply the good and appropriate response to being young, healthy, and attracted to others. I think this is an important point because too many young people assume or are taught that the sexual energy within them is evil, sinful, or inappropriate. The result is a massive amount of suppression, guilt, and/or shame connected to their bodies and their sexuality. *Sexual excitation does not equal lust.* While I admit that what precisely constitutes lust may not be easy to define, equating excitation with lust defies all levels of reason and Scripture.

Second, I want to communicate very clearly that every sexual act, no matter how trivial you perceive it to be, shapes you in ways beyond your current understanding. Therefore, any sexual behaviour outside of marriage can jeopardize your ability to experience the fulfilling sex life God is preparing for you within marriage (and by "sexual behaviour" I mean anything that involves the genitals—intercourse, oral sex, anal sex, mutual masturbation, etc.). Many couples deal with the fallout of previous sexual activity for years and even *decades* after they get married. It's helpful to remind ourselves again that on your wedding day God doesn't hit some kind of reset button and enable the two of you to enter into marriage with a blank slate. Marriage isn't magical. You bring all the good, bad, and ugly you've accumulated over your life into it. Don't jeopardize a future of great sex for a quick moment of pleasure now.

Third, if you do make a mistake and falter sexually, learn from your experience. It's true that all sexual acts before marriage have a negative influence on us, but there's an asterisk attached. That asterisk is this: God can and will bring restoration and healing for those who genuinely repent and recalibrate their lives to God's intentions for their bodies and their sexuality. While I do not believe we will experience God's redemptive power in our lives if all we're seeking is "cheap grace"[23], for those who are truly heartbroken over their sin and are committed re-establishing personal dignity within the sexual dimension of their lives, God will move in extraordinary ways. The healing and restoration may not occur as quickly as we'd like (or through the path we'd prefer) but for those who turn to Jesus, sin and its effects never have the last word.

Lastly, as I alluded to above I think masturbation is an option for those who feel they need a sexual outlet. While some see masturbation as an activity which increases lust and the desire for more sexual activity, I believe it can be used as a tool to *decrease* both. However, I also caution (as I did above) that defaulting to masturbation too often will not develop the character and habits that will help your sexual relationship within marriage to flourish. Therefore, I would argue that masturbation should only be viewed as a last resort, and should never be done while using pornography or other sexually stimulating material.[24] In bringing up the option of masturbation I'm aware of the complexities involved. It may appear as though I'm attempting to provide a justification for an

---

23 "Cheap Grace" is Dietrich Bonhoeffer's term which describes the flippant attitude of Christians in his day to sin and repentance. Regardless of the sin, Bonhoeffer noted that many Christians believed they could essentially just say "oops, sorry God" and then start over. In *The Cost of Discipleship*, Bonhoeffer writes "cheap grace is grace without discipleship, grace without the cross, grace without Jesus Christ."

24 I meet more people (young and old) who want to discuss the positive benefits of pornography. However, I cannot envision any scenario where the viewing of pornography is beneficial or appropriate, regardless of whether someone is single, dating or married. Pornography, while sexually exciting, is destructive in all of its forms. It always leads to a dehumanized view of sex and the human body, which for me makes all forms of pornography completely anti-Christian and incompatible with a discipleship commitment to Jesus.

activity that seems—in and of itself—to be a direct violation of Jesus' command to avoid lustful fantasies (Matthew 5:28). However, I do think it is problematic to assume *all* masturbatory behaviour is lust-filled. I can envision states of the heart and imagination that are neither lustful in their intent nor self-serving in their ends. Pastorally, I am also shaped by two pressing demands: the need to help move people into a more passionate and authentic discipleship commitment to Jesus, and the recognition that this is a process. Therefore, I believe that sometimes giving in to sexual urges and masturbating may be a sign of growth and maturity (e.g., months before this same person may have had sex with a friend). The realization that discipleship is a process emboldens me to suggest that some may find masturbation to be a helpful tool for a particular stage of their discipleship journey.

Top Relationship Advice

Even though this chapter is specifically looking at the issue of sex, most of the challenges we come up against sexually are directly related to our involvement in unhealthy relationships. Generally speaking, sexual mistakes tend to result from being in relationships that violate basic principles that lead to health, joy, and fulfillment. That's why I also spend time each year offering relationship advice to our students and young adults. If we want to cultivate a healthy sexuality, we need to cultivate healthy relationships. Over the years I've put together a list of what I consider to be the top relationship advice. The list has emerged through countless conversations and discussions, and offers some great ground-level wisdom on how the call of discipleship should steer our journey through romantic relationships. This is not a list where it's all or nothing—that is, in order to be a disciple, all of these ideas need to be in place. It's important to remember that discipleship is a process and a journey. Those who have taken to heart even one or two of these principles have told me that it has had a dramatically positive effect on their life, and has helped immensely in the process of controlling their negative sexual habits and impulses.

Keep your passion for Jesus central. It's easy to give Jesus priority status when there's no competition. When we start dating, however, it's common for many of us to slowly channel the energy that we've been investing in our relationship with him into our new found love. But Jesus isn't our relational back-up plan; someone we put first until someone better comes along. He needs to stay central for us regardless of whether we're single, dating, or married.

Relationships flourish when Jesus and his kingdom are the priority of both people, but falter when they aren't. When Jesus is our first priority our view of love, sex, and relationships is enhanced and enriched. But when Jesus is relegated to being our second, third, or fourth priority, our entire view of love, sex, and relationships becomes distorted. Knowing Jesus intimately is critical if we want to know what authentic, life-giving expressions of love, sex, and relationships look like. If we're not anchoring our heart's deepest hopes and longings in Jesus, our romantic relationships will always end up disappointing and frustrating us. We'll be placing unrealistic expectations on our relationship that can only be fulfilled by God.

It's a wonderful thing to fall in love and find someone with whom we can share our lives. However, we need to be careful that even good, healthy dating relationships don't become stumbling blocks that cause us to forsake our first love (Revelation 2:4).

Don't rationalize an abusive relationship. It's common for many people (especially women) to find themselves in an abusive relationship at some point in their lives. Maybe it's a boyfriend who is physically abusive, or a girlfriend who is controlling and emotionally manipulative. Regardless, I often see the rationalizing of major dysfunction happen all the time. Many of us would rather put up with abuse and dysfunction in our relationships that be alone, so we go to great lengths to minimize or deny any abusive behaviour.

"Well, she's not like that *all* the time."

"It isn't really *that* bad."

"It's not big deal. That's just the way our relationship is."

No relationship is perfect. Each one has its fault lines and issues, but there comes a point when a challenging relationship becomes a destructive one, and when abusive patterns have emerged, that line has been crossed.

Sometimes denial can run deep. If we don't identify and end the abusive relationship until it has run its course we will be heartbroken and devastated. Or maybe we believe we're the one sent into this person's life to do the saving, to make them a better person, and so we wear the abuse as a kind of badge of honour. Maybe it brings us some kind of self-righteous satisfaction that we're suffering for a greater purpose and are willing to love someone so "complicated."

Regardless of your particular situation, if you are involved in an abusive relationship (whether the abuse is physical, emotional, or sexual), you need to end it. You know it's unhealthy, and chances are it's negatively impacting every area of your life, including your relationship with God. You should talk to a friend, parent, or pastor who you trust and who can help you transition out of your relationship.

Don't believe that romantic relationships are the key to happiness and fulfillment. This piece of advice often comes from one of my high school students when we brainstorm relationship advice together as a group. All of us go through a stage where we assume we're a boyfriend or girlfriend away from having it all. We believe that if we could find our "true love" all the issues that bring us down would fade into the background; that love, peace, and joy would flood into our lives and give us our "happily ever after."

Falling in love and being in love is awesome, but if we think a relationship is what will save us from loneliness, low self-esteem, purposelessness, etc., we're just wrong. No matter how good, godly and healthy a relationship may be, it cannot fully satisfy the deeper, spiritual hungers within you. To enter into any relationship with the expectation that it will be the key to a happy life is to place an idolatrous, unhealthy, and unrealistic expectation on it. This expectation will only suffocate any potential for the relationship to grow in a healthy way. We must never ask or assume another person can provide what only God can. When we stop looking to a relationship to be the key that will unlock our lives, we open up space for healthy relationships to emerge into what they are meant to be.

Only date someone who has a passion for following Jesus with their whole lives. "Christians should only date Christians." That opinion is repeated in countless books on Christian dating, and yet from my point of view, it's just not a helpful way of approaching things. The statement is clearly well intended, but like many things within the church the attempt to simplify in order to communicate things clearly has created new problems.

For example, the overly simplistic categories of Christian and non-Christian can be an enormous stumbling block. If the discussion centres on dating Christians vs. non-Christians, we can quickly (and mistakenly) substitute "people who go to church" with "Christian" and unintentionally lower our standards to anyone who shows up to church on Sunday. But should a Christian relationship be validated by something as trivial as church attendance?

I think it's much better to frame the discussion within the larger context of discipleship. If we want our central passion to be Jesus and his kingdom, does it make sense to date someone that doesn't share that same intention? If discipleship to Jesus is something we take incredibly seriously, does it make sense to date someone who supports us in our faith, but isn't actually committed to it themselves?

No, it doesn't. That's why I encourage people to pray for and seek out someone whose passion for Jesus is profound, undeniable, and inspiring. That is the kind of person, that kind of disciple, is someone you should pursue. Too many people settle for someone who's churched instead of prayerfully holding out for someone whose discipleship commitment expresses itself in dynamic, passionate, creative ways. If you want your love for Jesus to deepen throughout your life, committing to only dating (and eventually marrying) someone with a strong and vibrant faith is a non-negotiable.

Never settle. Personally and professionally I've never, ever, ever seen anything good come from relationships that started with, "Well… you'll do." That being said, I'm not an idiot; I know how difficult it is to be the only person without a boyfriend or girlfriend, and the ache that situation creates. But we need to have the courage to move into and through that discomfort, trusting that God can somehow satisfy what we're longing for, even if we can't anticipate how.

Make a list of qualities you want in your future spouse, then work backwards. If you want someone who is fun, spontaneous, spiritually intense, wise, and playful, that's not going to happen if you date someone who is some of these things, some of the time. Obviously this means that we'll have to do a bit of reflection on our future marriage partner before we start dating, but isn't that a good thing? We date in order to allow God to help us find a kindred spirit with whom we can become a soul mate through marriage. If someone told me they were ready to date but couldn't articulate what they were looking for in someone beyond being attractive and funny, I'd tell them they just aren't ready to date. If we don't know what we really want in our dating relationships, the likelihood of us settling for something "good enough" is exponentially higher.

Before I met my wife I spend a few months putting together a list of character qualities that I wouldn't budge on when selecting the next person to date. If someone had 3 out of 10, I wouldn't date them. 8 out of 10? Sorry. I wanted a perfect score. Why? Was I some kind of unreasonable jerk with an inflated sense of entitlement? No. I knew what kind of marriage I wanted, and I'd lived and learned enough about myself to know the kind of person I needed to hold out for. That didn't make times of singleness easy, but because I had a razor-sharp clarity about what I wanted and needed, settling for anything else became much harder.

Avoid the Romeo and Juliet syndrome. Romeo and Juliet were the star-crossed lovers who were so in love they could never be separated. They quickly melted their own identities into each other and made each other their entire world. This syndrome is all too common in dating relationships. We've probably all known a friend who started dating someone and then stopped hanging out with everyone except their new love. All their spare time was spent with their Romeo or Juliet, and the relationships and priorities that were previously very important were disregarded and pushed aside.

The Romeo and Juliet syndrome is closely linked to the assumption that was addressed previously in this list (i.e., romantic relationships are the key to happiness and fulfillment). Out of this assumption we look to another person to be the emotional saviour we've been waiting for, and we do all we can to surround ourselves with this person as much as possible. This trap is easy for all of us to fall into, so my advice here is to put limits on the amount of time we're spending with our boyfriend/girlfriend, so that we don't (intentionally or unintentionally) make them the focal point of our daily routines and habits.

Set boundaries. It's really important to establish boundaries before we enter into a dating relationship. If we don't we'll find ourselves in a literal free-for-all in terms of what is done, said, and experience together, and this is always destructive to everyone involved. Healthy relationships need boundaries, and they need to identify and decide what boundaries are going to be in place as it relates to four dimensions of the relationship:

a. Physical. What physical boundaries need to be in place in order to protect each person's dignity, reputation, and purity?

b. Emotional. What emotional boundaries need to be in place in order to ensure the Romeo and Juliet syndrome doesn't take hold?

c. Social. What social boundaries need to be in place in order to ensure that each person is investing in healthy relationships outside of the dating relationship?

d. Spiritual. What spiritual boundaries need to be in place in order to ensure that each person is growing spiritually as individuals and not just focusing their spiritual growth on the context of their relationship?

Ideally, the couple should meet with a few older and more experienced couples to help them define what boundaries will be in place for them. These older couples can also play an important ongoing mentoring role in the new couples' lives.

Learn from your mistakes. We all make mistakes. As much as we parade around ideas of personal holiness, the biting truth is that imperfections and blunders seem to be the rule rather than the exception within our lives. Even during seasons where I feel an uncommon clarity of purpose, strong sense of conviction, and deep connection with God, I'm ashamed to admit how easy I'm seized by sins like lust, envy, pride, and idolatry.

But as I look back over my life, it seems to me that the only sinful slip-ups that have really cost me in the long run, have been the ones I've stubbornly repeated, knowing precisely what I was doing. Proverbs 26:11 states that "As a dog returns to its vomit, so a fool repeats his folly." That's the cycle that can destroy us if we're not careful. So when we make a mistake, regardless of what kind or what severity, we need to realize that beating ourselves up is of limited value. Genuine repentance doesn't always need to be a tearful exercise in self-pity. Sometimes it expresses itself with a clear decision and focused intention to put together a game plan to avoid repeating the mistake again. After reflecting on my own journey and many years of pastoral ministry, I'm convinced that God won't let our mistakes define our lives if we're willing to learn from them and seek restoration in Him.

Take three months between dating relationships to reflect and learn. The temptation to rebound with an immediate dating relationship after one has ended is enormous. Why? Because we've been in a relationship long enough that we've become accustomed to having someone to call, touch, and hang out with. To go from that to nothing feels like the rug has been pulled out from under us, and our first instincts are to get ourselves back into a relationship as soon as possible in order to avoid the awkwardness of readjusting to being single. But when we start relationships in order to avoid being single, we're actually just using the new guy or girl for our own selfish ends. That foundation isn't going to take us very far, and we should expect more heartache to come if we just rush into new relationships after ending old ones.

If a relationship doesn't work (for whatever reason), it's always important to take some time away from dating relationships and recalibrate our hearts and minds. We need to carve out time to reflect on what went wrong, and why. We should explore how we need to grow from our experiences in the previous relationship so that future relationships are healthier and more Christ-centred. Relationships teach us a lot if we're willing to listen to the lessons. Be sure to carve out at least three months between dating relationships so that you can focus on learning whatever lessons God wants to teach you during your time of transition.

Break up well. This might be one of the most surprising and overlooked pieces of advice I share on the subject of building healthy relationships, but it's so important. Nothing tests the genuineness of our discipleship commitment to Jesus than our willingness to refuse to blame, badmouth, or hurt the other person during a break up.

A break up usually means a lot of hurt for everyone involved. Two people who once thought of each other as "true loves" now become enemies looking to strike back at each other. However, it's exactly in this new and awkward context that Jesus' challenge to love our enemies (Matthew 5:44) comes into play.

If we're the ones doing the breaking up, we need to do so in a way that minimizes the emotional damage for the other person. We're going to cause hurt, so we need to be as gentle, reasonable, and as kind as humanly possible. Being rejected is a horrible feeling, and we don't need to escalate those feelings (even if we think the other person deserves it). We should strive to be gracious and kind, and after the break up never speak badly about the other person.

If we're on the receiving end of the break up, the emotions that flood into our hearts are going to make it very easy for us to justify hatred and retaliation. We need to fight those impulses with everything in us. That doesn't mean minimizing how much it hurts to have someone dump us, it just means refusing to let the hurt we're feeling morph into a cancer of anger and bitterness. Getting dumped sucks, but striking back through hatred and retaliation won't provide the healing we're now looking for. That can only be found when we pour our energy into our relationship with the One who is "close to the brokenhearted and saves those who are crushed in spirit" (Psalm 34:18).

The Challenge of Communion

At its best this chapter gives you a basic framework from which to participate with God in shaping a healthy sexuality that honours Him as well as the body He has given you. That doesn't mean the ideas in this chapter are easy or convenient to hear. But if you've made it this far into the book, you're probably not someone who will give up because things aren't easy or convenient.

What we do with our bodies is of extreme importance to God. Jesus told us to love God with all our strength (Mark 12:30). Part of what is implied there is to love God with how we use our bodies and our sexuality.

In Ephesians 5:31-32 Paul uses the sexual union within marriage as a metaphor for understanding Christ's relationship with the church. While such a metaphor may strike us as inappropriate or perhaps even obscene, Scripture invites us to reflect on how the passion and longing Christ has for his church is mirrored through the sexual embrace within marriage. In ways that might not seem obvious to us initially, our sexual urges are drawing us towards something more significant that we realize. We are physically longing for communion. That's one of life's big tests: will we commune with just anyone, or will we restrain ourselves so that we can enter into a sexual embrace that saves us from genuine loneliness and ushers in blessing, pleasure, and peace?

Love, sex, and relationships are always a risk because they always involve us yielding to someone else in vulnerability and transparency. However, when they converge in the context of God's love and guidance, something powerful and transformative happens. That's why, however scary or difficult the risk may be, it is a beautiful one worth taking.

6 a voice in the wilderness

You know that the rulers of the Gentiles lord it over them,
and their high officials exercise authority over them. Not so with you.
Instead, whoever wants to become great among you must be your servant.

~ Matthew 20:25-26

Each of us possesses some degree of power through which we influence others. Some of us hold *formal* power because we hold a title such as pastor, school president, team captain, etc. By virtue of having this title alone we are given a greater degree of power over those under our (formal) authority. But whether or not we hold any *formal* power because of a title, all of us hold *informal* power. All of us have been given by God a sphere of influence and authority within our lives and relationships. To a greater or lesser extent each of us can influence those around us, which means we have power.

By being part of a group we have power to influence others within that group for better or worse. As members of a sports team we have the ability to influence all of our teammates, whether or not we're the captain. It's the same within our friendships, dating relationships, family relationships, etc. We have a certain degree of power and we are always using it to influence others.

Think about that. Every moment of every day we are participating in relationships and networks of power. When we grasp the reality of that truth there is a demanding question we're confronted with as disciples of Jesus: *how are we using our power?* Becoming aware of the dynamic of power in our lives is an important first step, but once we begin to see how relationships of power shape our lives we need to confront our own use of the power God has entrusted to us. This is so critical because most of the suffering, injustice, and brokenness we see in the world is directly tied to abuses of power. In fact, all of the injustices that humans inflict on one another involve someone either applying or withholding their power to sexually, socially, economically, relationally, or emotionally exploit and harm others. Bullying, hate crimes, economic oppression, rape, spousal abuse, personal betrayal, etc., are all different expressions of the same root sickness: an abuse and misuse of power.

But there is good news. Scripture is full of insights that can teach us how to move towards wise and good uses of power. For example many of the laws in the Old Testament that seem boring or irrelevant are explicitly given by God to ensure that power is used in ways that bring life and hope instead of oppression, corruption and death. The Old Testament prophets are almost continually confronting God's people (or their pagan neighbours) on their abuses of power. In fact, the more I read and study the gospels the more convinced I am that Jesus is almost always in dialogue with the issue of power. Throughout his interactions with others he's continually confronting abuses of power (often committed by those with formal religious authority!) and modeling what a godly and life-giving use of power looks like. But even those closest to Jesus failed to understand and imitate his call to wield power wisely. For two disciples in particular, the lure of power was tremendously seductive and got them into lots of trouble.

Sons of Thunder

The disciples James and John are introduced to us in Matthew 4:21. They were in a boat with their father Zebedee when Jesus called them to be disciples. James and John were probably quite young given the fact that Scripture highlights they were fishing with their father. The fact that James and John were not fishing on their own means they were probably still in the apprenticeship stage of their training, which normally occurred between the ages of 13-17.

In Mark 3:17 we read that Jesus gives these two young men the nickname "Boanerges," which means "sons of thunder." I used to assume this was a positive label, until I started to think about what thunder does. What does thunder do? It makes noise. That's pretty much it.

James and John are *noisemakers*; not an uncommon trait for teenage guys. They are guys who talk a big game; loudmouths that throw around words without wisdom. The nickname "sons of thunder" was not a compliment but a *condemnation*, and there are at least two stories that validate this claim. Coincidentally, both stories revolve around the issue of power.

The first is found in Mark chapter 10:

> *"Then James and John, the sons of Zebedee, came to him. 'Teacher,' they said, 'we want you to do for us whatever we ask.' 'What do you want me to do for you?' he asked. They replied, 'Let one of us sit at your right and the other at your left in your glory.' 'You don't know what you are asking,' Jesus said. 'Can you drink the cup I drink or be baptized with the baptism I am baptized with?' 'We can,' they answered. Jesus said to them, 'You will drink the cup I drink and be baptized with the baptism I am baptized with, but to sit at my right or left is not for me to grant. These places belong to those for whom they have been prepared.'"* (Mark 10:35-40)

Notice the start of their conversation with Jesus: "Teacher," they said, "we want you to do for us whatever we ask" (verse 35). James and John were disciples to the greatest rabbi of their day and yet they kicked-off the discussion with a request that Jesus do for them whatever they want.

They were looking for Jesus to be their personal genie. They wanted Jesus to use his power to grant their wishes, no strings attached.

Jesus was inappropriately gracious to them and asked what they wanted. They were very honest in their reply: "Let one of us sit at your right and the other at your left in your glory" (verse 37). To sit at the right and left of royalty was to hold the two positions of highest honour. So James and John were asking for *power*. They wanted to be Jesus' vice presidents and have all of the glory and authority they perceived to be a part of those positions. This exchange in Mark's gospel makes it clear that James and John were ambitious, and that their ambition centred around gaining power so they could make *their* lives easier.

The second story is found in Luke chapter 9. It's another encounter that reveals James and John's immature craving for power and authority over others.

> "As the time approached for him to be taken up to heaven, Jesus resolutely set out for Jerusalem. And he sent messengers on ahead, who went into a Samaritan village to get things ready for him; but the people there did not welcome him, because he was heading for Jerusalem. When the disciples James and John saw this, they asked, 'Lord, do you want us to call fire down from heaven to destroy them?' But Jesus turned and rebuked them." (Luke 9:51-55)

When James and John believed they had access to Jesus' power they were quick to suggest using it to destroy anyone who stood in their way (hardly the mark of a mature disciple). Notice that Jesus turns and rebukes them—Jesus' kingdom isn't built by destroying those who set themselves against it! Despite their discipleship status and proximity to Jesus, the "sons of thunder" still had a lot to learn about power and how to use it rightly.

These two stories are a good reminder that even passionate, sincere disciples can be deceived and derailed by the lust for power.

A Voice in the Wilderness

If James and John are two biblical examples that reveal an immature and self-centred approach to power, John the Baptist stands as a model for a mature and Christ-centred approach. John the Baptist had a perspective on life grounded in profound humility. While James and John spent time seeking power and prestige, John the Baptist sought something very different. Even before Jesus bursts onto the scene the Bible tell us that John was already very powerful. Crowds of people were coming to him and he was on the radar of the political establishment because of his sway over the Jewish people. However, it's interesting to note that his power came through *informal* authority. He had no title (other than the nickname "the baptizer"), no position, and no credentials, but God used John to influence a huge amount of people. John the Baptist was having a tremendous impact through his life and ministry, so much so that some people began to wonder if he might be the Messiah of Israel. Before this rumour could gain much momentum, however, John announces:

> *"I baptize you with water. But one more powerful than I will come, the thongs of whose sandals I am not worthy to untie. He will baptize you with the Holy Spirit and with fire."* (Luke 3:16)

Despite his popularity and influence John didn't let it go to his head. John saw himself as a nobody compared to Jesus. Now imagine how difficult it must have been for John to keep his ego in check while all of those people celebrated him and proclaimed him to be the Messiah of God! Can you imagine how the "sons of thunder" would have reacted to that kind of adulation and popularity? And yet John says to the crowds that compared to the One to come, he's just splashing around in water and doing party tricks.

When the crowds pressed John with the question of whether or not he was the Christ. John's response was clear and direct: "I am not the Christ" (John 1:20).

"So who are you?" they asked.

"I am the voice of one calling in the desert, 'Make straight the way for the Lord,'" John answered.

With all of his power, popularity, and influence, John summarized his entire life as one who *makes straight the way for the Lord*. To "make straight the way" was an expression used to suggest the idea of making something easy. It came from the experience of travelers having to walk miles and miles from one location to another. During such a journey there was nothing more frustrating for someone than having to trek through hillsides, mountains, and zigzagging routes. What a traveler wanted was a straight, direct path from point A to point B.

John saw his role as making it as easy as possible for people to get from wherever they were to Jesus. John didn't care about power. He didn't care about sitting at the right or left hand of Jesus. He didn't care about prestige or popularity. John wanted to use whatever power and influence he'd been given to "make straight" the way to Jesus. His heart's deepest desire was to do whatever it took to help people come into a saving relationship with Jesus.

John the Baptist didn't want notoriety. He didn't even want to *share* the spotlight with Jesus. At one point he said that Jesus must rise in prominence and power while he became less (John 3:30). It's not that John was *disinterested* in power—I believe John the Baptist was just as obsessed with power as James and John were. The difference lay in the fact that John the Baptist wanted to use his power to glorify Jesus instead of glorifying himself.

John the Baptist is an inspirational example of how to properly understand and wield power. I hope that God has placed the desire within you to become a disciple with a heart like John the Baptist. I hope you're willing to use whatever power God has given you (whether formal or informal) to "make straight" the path to Jesus. As we see the abuses of power that exist within our schools, churches, families, and workplaces, it's hard not to resign ourselves to apathy. But the answer is not to give up and assume power corrupts. John the Baptist is one example (we will find another one momentarily) that shows us that it *is* possible to hold power and use it in ways that bring healing, help, and hope to others.

Making Straight the Way

At the heart of all issues of power are issues of justice, and the decision to live justly should never be viewed as an option for a disciple of Jesus. It may sound idealistic and naïve to pursue justice, but the call of Christ demands that justice become a core value we integrate into every area of our lives.

Living justly means that we are committed to using our power in ways that serve others instead of ourselves. That commitment begins when we start to examine how we use the positions of influence and power God has given us. This process isn't easy, however, because through it we become aware of the ways in which we use our power to self-promote, to make *our* lives easier, to make the way straight for *ourselves* while simultaneously creating hardship for others. So we avoid honest self-reflection and instead confess other people's sins. But Jesus makes it clear that whatever the issue is, we start by cleaning up our own internal mess before we concern ourselves with the state of another's (Matthew 7:3-5).

So for the next month I challenge you to pray this prayer every day:

"God, please help me to see the power and influence I have, how I misuse it for my own self-serving ends, and how I could use it to bring healing and hope to others."

If you pray that prayer every day for a month, I'm confident God will answer it. As He begins to reveal the ways you use power, pay attention to how your character is being shaped through its use. Notice how you deepen your bitterness and anger the more you use your own power to bully, abuse, mock, discourage, and hurt others. Then notice how you deepen your joy and peace as you use your power to help, encourage, empower, and support others.

A Daily Ritual

Jesus doesn't give up on us despite our unfaithfulness to him. James and John are great examples of that truth. They started off as self-absorbed teenagers who were slowly transformed into great leaders within the early church. Exactly how this transformation occurred isn't entirely clear, but there's an interesting encounter involving Jesus that is only included in John's gospel. It was an encounter that I believe caused James and John to experience a paradigm shift related to their understanding of the purpose of power. In John 13 we read:

"It was just before the Passover Feast. Jesus knew that the time had come for him to leave this world and go to the Father. Having loved his own who were in the world,

he now showed them the full extent of his love. The evening meal was being served, and the devil had already prompted Judas Iscariot, son of Simon, to betray Jesus. Jesus knew that the Father had put all things under his power, and that he had come from God and was returning to God;" (John 13:1-3)

John begins the account by establishing that *all things* had been placed under Jesus' power. Jesus was now at the zenith of power and influence. Although I can't substantiate it, I truly believe that John, with tears in his eyes, wrote the next two verses while recollecting his early years as a power-hungry disciple who craved power over others.

"so he got up from the meal, took off his outer clothing, and wrapped a towel around his waist. After that, he poured water into a basin and began to wash his disciples' feet, drying them with the towel that was wrapped around him." (John 13:4-5)

John records that Jesus—*at the moment he had the power to do anything*—washed the disciples' feet. In the 1st century feet were considered the dirtiest part of the body. Some homes even employed a slave to wash the feet of guests, so to have a person of status and authority wash feet was unheard of! That's why Peter's response is understandable:

> *"He came to Simon Peter, who said to him, 'Lord, are you going to wash my feet?' Jesus replied, 'You do not realize now what I am doing, but later you will understand.' 'No,' said Peter, 'you shall never wash my feet.' Jesus answered, 'Unless I wash you, you have no part with me.'"* (John 13:6-8)

It was offensive to Peter that the most powerful person in the room would do the foot washing. It was just...*wrong*. Jesus deserved the highest place of honour, and if anything the disciples should have washed *his* feet! John continues:

> *"When he had finished washing their feet, he put on his clothes and returned to his place. 'Do you understand what I have done for you?' he asked them. 'You call me 'Teacher' and 'Lord,' and rightly so, for that is what I am. Now that I, your Lord and Teacher, have washed your feet, you also should wash one another's feet. I have set you an example that you should do as I have done for you. I tell you the truth, no servant is greater than his master, nor is a messenger greater than the one who sent him. Now that you know these things, you will be blessed if you do them.'"* (John 13:12-17)

Jesus told them that an example had been set for them (and for any disciples who would come after them). The example given by Jesus struck at the heart of the issue of power, and through it Jesus wanted to teach his disciples a critical lesson. The lesson was: When we are in a position of power, we're to see it as an opportunity to bless others by washing their feet (i.e., serving them in humility and love).

That's a totally different paradigm than the world offers regarding power. Many people long to secure a position of power so that they can make *their* lives easier; so that others can serve and bless *them*. Isn't that the point? Why go through all of the hard work involved in gaining power if you have to use it to serve others?

But Jesus shows us a different way that is anchored in using our power to make life better for others, not ourselves. Jesus tells us to leverage whatever influence we have and wash the feet of those around us. Of course what it means to "wash feet" is going to look different in different contexts. But, there is a common element to all genuine foot washing, and that is that we humble ourselves and use our power to bless someone else.

We wash feet when we help someone work through a problem they're wrestling with when we have more enticing things to do with our time. We wash feet when we help a co-worker who's having a bad week by taking on some of their responsibilities so they can take it easy. We wash feet when we encourage the rookie on the team, making him feel like an equal and not a second-class citizen due to his status. We wash feet when we organize a fundraiser in support of the downtrodden and oppressed, offering a challenge to the cynics of the world who wouldn't waste time or money on "lost causes." We wash feet whenever we use our God-given power to make others' lives better instead of worry about enhancing our own.

In my experience it has been through the commitment to washing the feet of others that Jesus has begun a fresh and truly transformative work in my own life. Candidly, the attitude James and John held towards power parallels my own more closely than I'd like to admit. But I'm learning the same lessons that changed James and John forever. I'm learning to understand that the power God has given me isn't there to make my life easier. I'm learning that I'm supposed to use my power to lift up Jesus' name and fame, not my own. I'm learning that when I use my power to wash the feet of others, God changes my heart and outlook in incredible ways.

Jesus never criticized those who held power, only those who *misused* it. Jesus' solution to the problem of the misuse of power wasn't to run from power as if it were evil or inherently corruptive. Instead he modeled a redemptive use of power that brought life, freedom, and joy to others.

We need to follow in his steps. As disciples we need to commit to using the power and influence God has given us to wash the feet of those around us. If we do, Jesus' grace and power will take hold of our lives in new and commanding ways.

Is that what we want? If it is, then let's start by asking ourselves this question: *whose feet do I need to wash today?* That question is critical, because the answer to it is the next step we need to take. Let's go and use our power to bless others instead of ourselves, so that Jesus can use our efforts to make straight paths to himself.

PART III into the kingdom

7 the four loves

To love at all is to be vulnerable. Love anything, and your heart will certainly be wrung and possibly be broken. If you want to make sure of keeping it intact, you must give your heart to no one, not even to an animal. Wrap it carefully round with hobbies and little luxuries; avoid all entanglements; lock it up safe in the casket or coffin of your selfishness. But in that casket – safe, dark, motionless, airless – it will change. It will not be broken; it will become unbreakable, impenetrable, irredeemable. The alternative to tragedy, or at least to the risk of tragedy, is damnation. The only place outside of Heaven where you can be perfectly safe from all the dangers and perturbations of love is Hell.

~ C.S. Lewis

In Part I we looked at what it means to be a disciple, why a disciple needs to confront dualism and the importance of struggling with our faith so we can own it for ourselves. In Part II we prepared ourselves to face the three great idols of money, sex, and power. In this final section we'll continue to take things down to the ground level and ask what discipleship to Jesus looks like in our everyday lives. I know personally how difficult it is to take intentions like "living for Jesus," "spiritual growth," and "biblical discipleship" and connect them to the realities I face each and everyday. That's why I've focused these final three chapters on providing a *plan* for how to grow as a disciple of Jesus in the day-to-day.

I also want to make sure that this plan is intuitive and helpful. I don't see it as a victory if you read through this book, get to the end and think, "Interesting stuff—but what now?" Like most people I need a way of thinking about discipleship that translates into something *real* in my life. I need a strategy that helps me connect the dots between what I should do and how to do it. Too many Christian teachers peddle hype and emotionalism, offering inspiration without instruction. You and I don't need more Christianeze hype, we need a guide for daily discipleship.

Simply Christian

When confronted by those who sought to determine his yoke[25] and test his orthodoxy as a 1st century rabbi, Jesus faced a critical question: "What is the greatest commandment?" (Mark 12:28). If we were asking that question today we might rephrase it by saying, "What

---

25 A rabbi's yoke was a combination of several worldview elements including their unique teaching style, philosophy of ministry, expectations for followers, and their understanding of the Torah and its most essential features and demands.

is the most important thing in life?" The question posed to Jesus came from a recognition that not all priorities are equally weighted, and Jesus' listeners wanted to know what single foundation was the best one on which to build their lives. The answer Jesus gave was: "Love the Lord your God with all your heart and with all your soul and with all your mind and with all your strength" (Mark 12:30).

To love God with one's entire being was the established answer for any God-fearing Jew, and no one in Jesus' day expected to hear differently. Jesus and those who came to follow Him as disciples were shaped by the conviction that what mattered most could be distilled into a few words: Love God. Heart. Soul. Mind. Strength.

Basic stuff right? This is one of the lessons you learn if you grow up in church, or learn within weeks of becoming a Christian. It's recognized by every Christian tradition as the foundational command for the Christian life. But how do we actually love God heart, soul, mind, and strength? One thing is clear, and that is that many of us are not doing it. The purposeful pursuit of loving God heart, soul, mind, and strength isn't a daily reality for many Christians.

Would anyone think it's even *probable* that if you were to ask ten strangers on the street what they associated with the word "Christian," their responses would be overwhelmingly positive? I doubt it. What matters most to Jesus simply hasn't taken root in the lives of those who call him their Lord.

When I dwell on that fact, my first reaction is to chastise the Christian community (myself included) for not taking Jesus' words seriously enough. But is it really just a matter of spiritual apathy? Is the solution to shame ourselves into taking Jesus more seriously? Are we just too lazy, stupid, affluent, or selfish as Christians—is that the root of the problem? Maybe. However I'm convinced it's just as likely that no one has ever taught us what it means to love God heart, soul, mind, and strength in the daily realities of life, and how to do it.

I'm passionately committed to helping make discipleship to Jesus concrete and accessible to people, and that commitment has led me on an expedition to reclaim the importance of Jesus' highest priority, and come up with a plan that connects it to normal, everyday life.

The Four Loves

Over the past several years I've explored Jesus' command to love God heart, soul, mind, and strength through a psychological window. I majored in psychology during my undergraduate training and my studies helped me develop a perspective from which to approach this command: the perspective of *types*. Typologies classify people based on patterns and are common within psychology, and I remember wondering if contained within this simple command were four ways—four typologies—that could help me better understand how to grow as a disciple.

Some of you reading this may be familiar with the idea of love languages. That's the idea that within relationships each of us prefers to give and receive love in specific ways. For some, receiving gifts communicates love more deeply than words of praise. For others, a word of praise communicates love much more powerfully than receiving a gift.

One of the keys to healthy relationships is to understand your own love language and take the time to understand the love language of others within your life. That way you can express your love in ways that are deeply meaningful to them, while receiving meaningful expressions of love in return.

What holds true in human relationships also holds true in our relationship with God, and again and again I see this same love language principle playing itself out in people's relationship with Jesus. While each of us is capable of expressing all of the love languages described below, I believe that one of the four serves as foundational for our experience of God. Our first task as disciples is to identify that root type. Once we've identified our root type we should spend time strengthening and developing it. But we shouldn't stop there. After all, Jesus' command is to love God "with all of your heart, soul, mind, *and* strength," not "with all of your heart, soul, mind, *or* strength." Our calling is to eventually branch out and learn to love God in ways that don't come naturally to us. If we do we'll experience God in successively deeper and profound ways, and transformation in Christ will go from being a pious platitude to lived experience.

Type One: The Heart Type

To love God with all of one's *heart* is to find ourselves and our faith energized as we passionately invest in relationships. Those who fall within this type have a root experience of God that is directly linked to their experience with people. Heart types are usually sensitive, empathetic, enthusiastic, and compassionate. They tend to feel things very intensely and live and love out of a heightened sensitivity to the moods and emotions of others. They are often quick to involve themselves in activities that hold the promise of a substantial emotional or relational outcome.

Heart types look to Scripture primarily to deepen their sense of connection with God and to learn how to deepen their relationships with others. "By this all men will know that you are my disciples, if you love one another" (John 13:35) is an example of the kind of Scripture that a Heart type hears and says, "Yes! That's what it's all about!" They know that if we don't embed a love for God and others into everything we do we gain nothing (1 Corinthians 13:3). When talking about their faith Heart types gravitate towards word pictures that strike a more relational chord. They talk about their "personal relationship with Jesus" and describe their church community as "my family." They are often vulnerable and sensitive in relational contexts and this makes them valuable members to churches, where they are often appreciated for their relational gifts.

Heart types experience God most strongly during times of community and togetherness. From church socials to conversations before/after church, Heart types tend to find Sunday morning factors like the message or music far secondary to whether they feel connected to God and others during their time together. People and relationships make the difference for this root type. This is why many Heart types will stay at churches through all kinds of congregational dysfunction. The relationships that they have established are extremely valuable to them, and supersede whatever issues may be surfacing within their church context.

It's so important for Heart types to grow beyond their root because the temptation to identify God's presence and activity with their current emotional state is a strong one for them. For an immature Heart type, if they *feel* good, then God is good; if they *feel* depressed, God has abandoned them; if they *feel* they are growing, God must be at work in their lives. God does speak to us through our emotions, but our emotions are not a reliable foundation for spiritual growth and discernment. Heart types must seek to grow in the other dimensions or they risk developing a spirituality that can hardly be distinguished from emotionalism. Emotionalism is a condition characterized by being "tossed back and forth by the waves, and blown here and there" (Ephesians 4:14) by the ups and downs of one's emotional experiences.

Type Two: The Soul Type

To love God with all of one's *soul* means we'll experience our love for God most acutely through times of reflection, meditation, solitude, and contemplation. At their best, Soul types are deep, grounded, centred, reflective, and wise. At their worst, they can become aloof, disconnected, and relationally distant. In general, Soul types find it much easier to live within the rhythms of the moment, and are better than other types at not worrying about the past or the future. They are at home in the moment and experience God through this posture.

The Scripture that best expresses the natural state of the Soul type is Psalm 46:10: "Be still, and know that I am God." For Soul types the past is formative and the future is possibility, but the *present* is the arena of transformation. Therefore, Soul types have a much easier time than the other types recognizing God's power and presence in the everyday moments that make up their lives. Enjoying a cup of tea, driving to work, reading a book, conversations with a friend, etc., are all activities that Soul types connect with God easily through.

Soul types are often more interested in loving God through hearing God and spending silent, reflective time in His presence. This lends itself to an attraction to contemplative practices ranging from journaling to silence retreats. While these practices are much more difficult for the other three types, the Soul type finds them to be stimulating and refreshing.

An interesting sidebar regarding the Soul type is that they often go unnoticed and unappreciated within many churches. This is because they often don't show up on the leadership's radar as "movers and shakers" and tend to make few demands on the community. They are often the antithesis of the classic Type A personality, so they are drawn to churches that give them space to live out their quiet (but not simple) faith in ways that allow them a certain level of anonymity. This means that many Soul types eventually leave energetic evangelical churches because these communities tend to emphasize a Christian spirituality that is grounded in one of the other three types.

Soul types must grow beyond their root or the desire to remove themselves from the rhythms of regular life may become a problem. The Soul type longs to immerse themselves in prayer and reflection. This immersion, however, can become a rationalization that promotes a privatized spirituality that moves them away from realities that should be faced. The core temptation for the Soul type is to extract themselves from the world so that they can pursue a deeper, unpolluted experience of God. But that movement is anti-Christ. We do not find God by detaching from His creation. We experience the richness of God as we embrace the struggles and challenges that are part of living in God's good world.

Christians famously speak of aiming to be *in* the world, but not *of* the world, but if the Soul type doesn't learn to love God with their heart, mind, and strength as well, they may find themselves *detached* from the world and unable to impact it as a disciple.

Type Three: The Mind Type

To love God with all of one's *mind* is to find our love for God energized as we grow in biblical knowledge, insight, and wisdom. Mind types are drawn to activities that increase their theological knowledge and expand their worldview. Their experience and engagement within churches is almost completely tied to the teaching ministries within the church. Because of this, Mind types tend to evaluate their own growth by assessing what they've learned lately, what new insights they've been given, and how their biblical knowledge has deepened.

Those who fall within this type are more aware than the other types that "Man does not live on bread alone, but on every word that comes from the mouth of God" (Matthew 4:4). It is very hard for Mind types to go more than a day or two without some form of mental stimulation and challenge. This can be a burden to those around them because the expression of such intellectual intensity can be experienced as unrelenting and exhausting.

Perhaps the most common stereotype for Mind types is that they are too conceptual and impractical—"too heavenly minded to be any earthly good" as the saying goes. While this criticism may be overstated, Mind types do validate this statement more than the other types. It is easy for Mind types to become absorbed with theological and philosophical issues while inadvertently ignoring the practical demands of their daily responsibilities.

Mind types face a challenging discipleship journey (I know because I'm a Mind type). If they simply stay in their root type and ignore the call to learn to love God with their heart, soul, and strength, it can become all too easy for them to spend their lives *thinking* about God without living *for* and *with* God. They are at more risk than the other types to stay trapped in their head. They can become obsessed with ideas and orthodoxies (i.e., right teaching), but never move into the orthopraxis (i.e., right living) that they need for transformation.

Immature Mind types are argumentative and critical, and often see themselves as spiritually superior to others due to having "correct" theology. This can be especially true in evangelical churches, because these communities often hold up Mind types as the role models for what discipleship should look like. Those who know the Bible, know their theology and are skilled in articulating it are celebrated and revered. Because of this, it's a difficult and ego-bruising journey for the Mind type to learn that their type is simply *one* of the types, and not *number one* of the types.

Type Four: The Strength Type

To love God with all of one's *strength* is to find one's faith energized as one uses their physical energy to serve and bless others in practical ways. Strength types focus on pragmatic acts of generosity and kindness and find these especially rewarding and meaningful. Strength types have a genuine understanding that the movement from being a "hearer" to "doer" (James 1:22) is critical for discipleship and faith. Strength types are often models to the other types in showing what living out one's faith looks like in concrete ways.

Many Strength types have difficulty getting anything out of Scripture unless it is tied directly to a practical application. While other types (especially Mind types) are busy trying to understand what Scripture is teaching them, Strength types are asking, "What should we *do* about it?" From the conceptual to the concrete: that is always the movement for Strength types.

Within their churches Strength types are invaluable. They are often well known and deeply appreciated due to the fact that they are the doers of the church, the 20% that seems to accomplish 80% of the work. They are passionate servers that rarely seek recognition or reward. Serving others *is* the reward for a Strength type because they love to offer help in practical ways to those around them.

If growth in the other dimensions of loving God is not pursued by Strength types, the stereotype of the do-gooder can come true. This can lead to a discipleship that is divorced from depth at the theological, relational, and contemplative levels. Without these other dimensions being explored it can also become easy for Strength types to define their spiritual health with their level of activity and good works. This can cause Strength types to become workaholics that are fuelled by an unhealthy urge to constantly busy themselves with many godly things. That was Martha's temptation in Luke 10:38-42. She was busy serving Jesus (strength), but needed to learn to be still before him (soul), learn from him (mind), and deepen her relationship with him (heart).

A Plan for Discipleship

The simplest definition of a disciple that I can think of is this: someone who is taking Jesus' command to love God heart, soul, mind, and strength seriously. In order to do that we need to first identify our root type and nurture it. To experience and love God in the way we do is a gift and we should celebrate it! What I love about Jesus' command, however, is that it pushes us beyond the borders of what comes naturally. One of the four loves will come naturally to us—that isn't the problem. The problem comes when we become satisfied with living out of our root type and miss out on the adventure of discovering the greatness of God as we learn to love Him in more holistic ways.

It is difficult for Heart types to conduct a systematic study of the Bible, but at some point this type needs to take up this challenge so that they learn to love God with their mind as well as their heart. Likewise, it's not easy for Strength types to participate in contemplative practices, but discipleship demands that such a challenge be attempted. After all, a root is supposed to nurture something greater than itself, and our root type is there to be the starting point from which our love for God can become more robust and expansive.

So how do we put all of this together into a plan for daily discipleship? Three steps are necessary:

1. Do one activity *every day* that strengthens your root type. Whatever your type, nurture it daily by doing an activity that strengthens your personal love language with God.

2. Do one activity *every week* that falls within a different type. For example, if you're a Strength type choose one Heart, Soul, and Mind activity for the week. It doesn't have to be something huge or radical, but you should set a goal to do one activity each week that stretches you beyond your comfort zone. [26]

3. As you grow in loving God with all of your heart, soul, mind, and strength, look for ways to extend that love into your relationships with others. Jesus said the second most important thing is to love your neighbour as yourself, and out of our experience

---

26 For ideas on how to grow within each type please visit www.meredisciple.com for a free .pdf download.

and understanding of God's love, our lives will overflow with compassion, care, and justice for others.

I use these steps on a weekly basis. At the beginning of each week I sit down and think about how I'd like to try to stretch myself in loving God heart, soul, mind, and strength. I take the time to set a goal for myself within each type. For example, last week I came up with the following plan:

Heart: Set aside some time to connect with a friend I haven't talked to in a while. Really listen and try to discern God's movements in his life. Offer encouragement and support.

Soul: Journal once this week on something God seems to be challenging me with.

Mind: Complete my study on Colossians this week and take notes on anything that stands out.

Strength: Help the set-up team on Sunday morning this week at church.

As you can see, in each area I've tried to identify one thing that I could do within the next week that would stretch me beyond my preferred love language. Some weeks I come up with more than one thing for each area, but I try not to worry about quantity; I just try to think about one way I can learn to grow in my love for God heart, soul, mind, and strength.

Mere Discipleship

I'll be the first to admit that this model isn't complex. In fact, it's rather simplistic. But that doesn't mean it's easy. If you challenge yourself to go through this process at the start of every week I think you'll find it more difficult than you'd imagine it to be. It will be easy to come up with a goal when it comes to your root type, but for the other three (and especially your weakest love language) you may find it frustrating. You'll learn very quickly how easily you default to what comes naturally to you in your relationship with God.

But it's important to push through whatever frustrations you encounter. Jesus lived out of a balanced and perfect expression of these four love types. Take the time to read through the gospels and observe how Jesus expressed the four loves through his life and ministry. You'll notice Jesus modelled all of them and challenged others to stretch themselves beyond their root type.

One of the other things that I can't stress enough is that this discipleship plan really only works in the context of Christian community. You and I need to rub shoulders with those who love and experience God differently than we do. It's through the interaction with other types that we learn that *our* type is not *the* type. With this realization our appreciation for the different types within Jesus' church increases (1 Corinthians 12:2). Through my participation in my own church community, I've grown to deeply appreciate those who love God in ways that seem foreign or uncomfortable to me. It's so easy within the Christian subculture to let yourself gravitate to those of the same age, life-stage, or type. But courageous discipleship pushes us into a context that demands more from us; a context that isn't tailored to our wants and desires, but one that is tailored to our growth and maturity.

Loving God heart, soul, mind, and strength is an evolving and exciting journey. I've been using this model in my own life for a relatively short period of time, but the results have been tremendous. Jesus' central command has inspired me to explore the unique possibilities that only come from stretching myself to move beyond loving God with my mind and learning from those for whom the heart, soul, or strength dominate. I've learned that if I make small attempts to grow in each of the four loves, I can expect to experience God in surprising, beautiful, and transformative ways.

8 tikkun olam

But nothing worth having ever comes without a fight
Got to kick at the darkness till it bleeds daylight.

~ Bruce Cockburn

There is a resurgence happening within the global Christian community, and it's focused on the word *justice*. When I became a Christian in grade nine, for the first 5-7 years I learned a lot about the Christian faith. I learned about the importance of worship, prayer, serving others, attending church, and reading the Bible. I was blessed to have some key foundational elements of the faith drilled into my emerging Christian worldview. However, I'm sad to say that I never once remember being taught about the biblical call to justice. God's commands to seek justice (Isaiah 1:17) and look after orphans and widows (James 1:27) were conspicuously absent from the evangelical teaching and literature I was exposed to.

Today, we hear about justice issues like the human trafficking, government sponsored genocide, and extreme poverty all the time. As our world becomes increasingly smaller, we're becoming more aware of the issues that keep God's world in bondage, and are being challenged to right those wrongs.

While it's great to see our awareness of these issues increasing, I'm troubled by my suspicion that many Christians—including myself—still hold to a very soft and domesticated concept of justice. It's become very *en vogue* to talk about justice or hawk one's favourite cause on Facebook. However, I wonder how many of us have really done the hard work of trying to discern the implications that a commitment to justice would hold for us. If we don't anticipate those implications and consequences, whatever present progress is being made to promote justice is going to burn out and be remembered as a trend of the early 21st century. Movements that last and transform the world are often ignited by a keyword, but they aren't sustained by one. Movements always have to go deeper or else today's rallying concept becomes tomorrow's trite nostalgia. So as we explore what it means to be a disciple of Jesus in the midst of our everyday lives, we need to deepen our understanding of what justice is and what it calls us to do and become. We can't let the countless justice initiatives that have emerged burn out, because the causes are too vital and too much is at stake.

The Heart of Justice

Justice is something that is extremely important to God. In Deuteronomy 16:20 God calls His people to, "Follow justice and justice alone" and Isaiah 56:1 commands us to, "Maintain justice and do what is right." In Jeremiah 21 God instructs us to:

> "Administer justice every morning; rescue from the hand of his oppressor the one who has been robbed, or my wrath will break out and burn like fire because of the evil you have done—burn with no one to quench it."
> (Jeremiah 21:12)

In one of the most well-known Scriptures summarizing God's call for humans to live justly, the prophet Micah proclaims:

> "He has showed you, O man, what is good. And what does the Lord require of you? To act justly and to love mercy and to walk humbly with your God." (Micah 6:8)

In many ways, the issue of justice is embedded into every page and story in the Bible. From Genesis to Revelation, one of the great themes of Scripture is that God is bringing His restorative justice to His creation, righting the wrongs we've committed. Justice is clearly important to God, but what exactly is it?

My definition of the biblical concept of justice is very simple: *justice is fighting to make things right.* God is a God who fights to make things right and He wants His people to fight for the same thing. This begs the question: is that kind of justice something you value as a disciple of Jesus? Do you *fight* for what is right?

"Yeah, I think people should do the right thing."

That's not what I asked. Do you *fight* for what is right?

Justice means more than just doing the right thing. It often means *fighting on behalf of those who are being mistreated.* People are being mistreated in our schools, our neighbourhoods, our homes, our cities, and our churches—are we *fighting* for them?

"Well, I'm not hurting them," you may object. But it's not enough to not hurt others. That's being *nice.* That's being *civil.* That's not being *just.* Being nice and being civil means you're not part of the problem. Being just means you're part of the solution. Jesus calls us to be both, but too often Christians focus on the former and ignore the latter.

Too many Christians think it's good enough not to bully; but we're also called to stand between the bully and the victim.

Too many Christians think it's good enough not to steal; but we're also called to help restore the victim of theft.

Too many Christians think it's good enough not to have sex before marriage; but we're also called to offer compassion and hope to those who have.

Too many Christians think it's good enough to avoid drugs; but we're also called to help rescue those who are in bondage to drug addictions.

Too many Christians think it's good enough to simply not make things worse. But God's call of justice sets a higher standard. You're called to fight to make things better.

Let me be very honest here. I've thought about this a lot. I think that if someone said that Jeff Strong was a person committed to this kind of justice, I'd be very uncomfortable with that assertion. You know why? I've spent most of my Christian life being *nice* to people. I've done my best not to hurt, steal, or make things worse for others. But I'm not sure if I can say I've *fought* to make things right for those who have been wronged.

Have I fought for the single mothers around me who have been victimized and feel hopeless and lonely? Have I fought for that student at my school that everyone picks on? Have I fought to befriend the person everyone else sneers at or ignores? Have I fought for the immigrants in my city who are trying to rebuild lives torn apart by oppression back in their country of origin? Have I fought for the four year old girl who is used and abused as part of a human trafficking operation?

If I want to call myself a disciple of Jesus with any integrity, I need to start fighting for what is right. I need to start fighting to make things right for those who have been wronged.

Hidden in Plain Sight

It's mind-boggling and embarrassing to admit that I'm discovering God's call to justice sixteen years after becoming a Christian. How did that happen? If justice is so important to God and so critical to discipleship, why am I discovering it now? Why didn't I see it all along?

The biblical theme of justice is difficult to notice if you spend most of your time reading the New Testament like I did when I came to faith. That's because the word justice doesn't come up very often in the New Testament. Unless we have eyes to see it, it's possible to read through the New Testament over and over again and find ourselves reading about sin, salvation, sanctification, worship, but not justice. However, the concept is there, it's just hidden in plain sight.

As you make your way through the New Testament, what you do encounter again and again is the word *righteousness*. Righteousness is an extension of the Hebrew word *sedeq*, and English translations go one of two ways when they come upon this root. They'll either translate it as *right/righteous/righteousness* or *just/justice/justify*. That means that all of these words and concepts belong together linguistically and theologically. Said even more simply, *righteousness and justice are two different ways of saying the same thing.*

When I learned that, everything changed. It became a lot easier for me to see how important justice is for someone who's seriously trying to follow Jesus. Jesus' teachings challenged me in new ways as I took familiar passages that used the word righteous/righteousness and substituted justice. Here's one example:

> "So do not worry, saying, 'What shall we eat?' or 'What shall we drink?' or 'What shall we wear?' For the pagans

run after all these things, and your heavenly Father knows
that you need them. But seek first his kingdom and his
***justice**, and all these things will be given to you as well."*
(Matthew 6:33)

Jesus' teaching here takes on such a different tone when the word justice is used instead of righteousness. Here's another example: "Blessed are those who hunger and thirst for **justice**, for they will be filled" (Matthew 5:6). Jesus wants His church to be filled with people who hunger and thirst for justice; people who will make things right, whatever the cost to themselves.

As I re-read the New Testament through this lens, substituting the word justice for righteousness as I went along, I underwent a profound paradigm shift. The Old Testament started to take on new depth and significance as a result. I stopped seeing it as an extended list of rules and outdated stories, and began to see how justice was one of its major teaching points. As every page turned I found myself experiencing a renewed passion to rethink my assumptions about God's larger agenda within the world. I began to realize Jesus was leading me into a radically new space.

As I followed his lead, I began to realize that Jesus wasn't going to convert me into a nice person. He didn't need me to be nice, he needed me to be *just*. He was going to reform me into a fighter who mirrored God's pledge to be a "defender of widows" (Psalm 68:5) and one who encourages the oppressed (Isaiah 1:17). For the first time I began to see that Jesus' vision for the church wasn't a community of nice people who didn't do bad things. Jesus' vision was a community of justice-seekers who hungered to fight against the forces of oppression and darkness in the world.

Confronting the Chaos

There are two Jewish concepts that can immeasurably help us transition justice from an ideology to a daily expression of our love for God and others. The first is the concept of *chaos*. Within a Jewish worldview the opposite of God is not the devil, but chaos. Chaos is synonymous with meaninglessness, lack of purpose, disorder, and disharmony. When anything is out of sync with God's purposes and intentions it is in a state of chaos and disharmony. Throughout the Scriptures water is used as a symbol of chaos. In Genesis 1:2 we read that the Spirit of God was hovering over the waters—the formless chaos. The seas and oceans were always feared by God's people. This wasn't just because they posed a clear and present physical danger, but because the seas and oceans were believed to be the embodiment of chaotic, anti-God forces. The waters served as a reminder of the truth that where God is not, chaos and death reigns. Interestingly, a person whose life was in a state of chaos was said to be *poor*. The biblical definition of poverty, therefore, is a broad term that communicates the idea that someone's life (or a part of it) is in chaos and disruption. This is an important insight for us because it means when someone is called poor in Scripture, this isn't *necessarily* referring to their economic status. They may, in fact, have lots of money but find themselves in relational, social, mental, or spiritual chaos.

The second concept that builds upon the first comes from the mystic tradition within Judaism and is called *tikkun olam*. This is a Jewish expression that has been used to summarize God's plans and purposes for the world and humanity. *Tikkun* means "to fix or restore that which is broken," while *olam* means "the world." *Tikkun olam*, therefore, means *the restoration of a broken world*. That's almost the exact wording used in previous chapters of this book to describe God's redemptive mission within the world. As God's kingdom (i.e., God's power and presence) breaks forth on the earth, people are rescued from a state of chaos and delivered into a state of shalom (wholeness and harmony). This concept of *tikkun olam* fits the pattern of Jesus' ministry we find described in Matthew 4:

> *"Jesus went throughout Galilee, teaching in their synagogues, preaching the good news of the kingdom, and healing every disease and sickness among the people. News about him spread all over Syria, and people brought to him all who were ill with various diseases, those suffering severe pain, the demon-possessed, those having seizures, and the paralyzed, and he healed them."* (Matthew 4:23-24)

Matthew records that wherever Jesus went he brought about *tikkun olam*. Jesus continually moved people from a place of chaos to wholeness.

Where he found death, he brought life. Where he found desperation, he supplied hope. Where he found bondage, he offered freedom. Where he found suffering, he extended healing. In fact, almost every chapter contained within the gospels shows Jesus confronting chaos and replacing it with *tikkun olam*. That is why the message Jesus lived and taught is such good news! God is repairing the world through Jesus, and through Jesus we are invited to exchange the chaos in our lives for God's harmony, healing, and goodness.

As Christians, therefore, our task is to partner with God's agenda for *tikkun olam*. Individually we do this by asking how God wants to use us to fight chaos and extend *tikkun olam*. Collectively we do this by asking how the church can become a group of people who bring Jesus' love to those in chaos. If Jesus established the ministry blueprint of entering into the chaos in order to bring about *tikkun olam*, those who don't seek to follow his example can hardly be called disciples.

Instruments of Justice

Jesus is preparing us for a fight. Are we ready to take a beating for his glory? Are we ready to earn the bruises and battle scars that only come from fighting for justice in his name? If we are, then tomorrow take the first step and "offer yourselves to God, as those who have been brought from death to life; and offer the parts of your body to him as instruments of **justice**" (Romans 6:13). Let's start kicking at the darkness until it bleeds daylight.

But know that confronting the dark realities of our world won't be easy. It sounds heroic when it's preached from the pulpit and written about on a blog, but actually doing it is scary as hell. That's because a lot of the time that is exactly where Jesus leads us to: hell on earth. I think most of us recognize that, which is why we spend so much time *talking* about redemption and restoration, while avoiding the very places where they're needed most. Tim Hughes' song *God of Justice* is one of my favourites, but not because it's easy to listen to. It's actually very irritating and annoying. It strikes us right at the point where our intentions and ideals surrounding justice fail to connect with real life; the point where our self-preserving instincts shut things down. There's a haunting line in the chorus that asks God to "keep us from just singing: *we must go.*" Now maybe that's a Heart type struggle in particular, but the principle cuts across all lines.

The Soul type sings, "keep us from just praying: *we must go.*"

The Mind type sings, "keep us from just learning: *we must go.*"

The Strength type sings, "keep us from just doing: *we must go.*"

We all need to go. We need to go into the places where we'd rather not, because that's where Jesus went and where he still wants to go through his people.

Of course, we don't need to go very far before we find brokenness and chaos. If we're honest, there's more than enough within our own lives and hearts. Maybe God does want to use us to help save the world, but we're going to have to let God save us first. Save us from the pride, bitterness, anger, shame, loneliness—from whatever chaos is churning around in our souls.

How do we do that? How do we exchange our chaos for God's wholeness? Remember that Jesus is a Master at facilitating that exchange. We need to go to him and be honest about the brokenness within our lives. We need to ask him to do whatever he needs to do in order to bring us out of the chaos. We also need to look at our lives and "throw off everything that hinders and the sin that so easily entangles" (Hebrews 12:1) in order to create space for the Spirit to do its work within us. As God brings to completion the work He has begun in us, we then need to reach out to those around us who are in chaos.

Each of us is called into different places of chaos, but our common ground as disciples is that we're all called to do justice. Each of us is charged with the responsibility to fight for what is right and help bring about *tikkun olam*. It doesn't matter if you're a lawyer, part-time burger flipper, student, pastor, graphic artist, nurse, engineer, coach. Wherever God has placed us is where we need to start that fight and bring hope to those who are poor, crushed in spirit and hungry for hope.

9 a tree of life

For a tree there is always hope.

~ Job 14:7 (The Message)

In 2 Peter 3:18 we read: "But grow in the grace and knowledge of our Lord and Saviour Jesus Christ." I don't know about you, but "growing in the grace and knowledge of Jesus" sounds about as Sunday school and cliché as you can get. It would be on the shortlist of right answers to the question of what discipleship entails. We are encouraged to grow in this knowledge by our churches, our friends, and our families, but very few of these sources actually prepare us for the consequences this growth will hold for us. Between the ages of 18-25 those consequences begin to come into focus. We begin to realize that following Jesus will cost us more than we originally thought; that a strong and vibrant relationship with God won't translate into a consistent stream of warm fuzzies and spiritual highs.

C.S. Lewis observed that the greater the level of intimacy between two people, the more complicated the relationship becomes. If C.S. Lewis is right, that means that as our relationship with God matures and grows, it will simultaneously feel more complicated, confusing, and troublesome. Many of us would interpret those feelings as being evidence that something is very *wrong* in our relationship with God. But what if that assumption is mistaken? What if the complexity, confusion, and struggles are all signs of growth and maturity?

If you picture your relationship with God as a circle, one that enlarges as you grow in His grace and knowledge, you'll better understand how the experience of confusion and complexity is tied to your growth and maturity. As your circle of knowledge grows, *so does its outer edge of ignorance.*

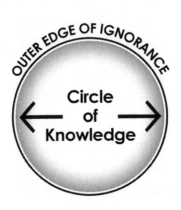

This explains why the most opinionated and inflexible Christians are usually those with the smallest circle of knowledge. They're full of certainties about God, life, relationships, etc., because their outer edge of ignorance is so small and static due to their lack of growth. On the contrary, those with a large circle of knowledge know a lot, but that knowledge drives them into a place of powerful humility because they are acutely aware of their expanding edge of ignorance. In other words, the more they know about God, they more they realize they don't know

Coming to the realization that you don't know as much about God and the Christian journey as you thought you did may feel overwhelming or perhaps even a little scary. But you need to brace yourself for that discomfort, because if you grow in the grace and knowledge of Jesus over the next few years, your worldview (your circle of knowledge) will explode relationally, spiritually, psychologically, intellectually, etc. You will not be able to predict how it will happen. You will not be able to predict when it will happen. You will not be able to control it. All of this will lead to an experience of intellectual/relational/spiritual vertigo, *but this is a sign of health and growth!* Maybe this scares you, maybe it excites you. But now you can begin to see the kind of courage it takes to follow the path of discipleship and grow in Jesus' grace and knowledge. It's a difficult and trying journey, but one that will lead to a life-altering experience of God.

An Enduring Hope

Growing in the grace and knowledge of Jesus will mean that

we'll have to face trials and hardships in order to push us forward and deepen our faith. In order to ensure times don't slowly grind us down and embitter us, we need an enduring hope; a source of continuous encouragement and empowerment. As we invest in our relationship with God, hope becomes one of the pivotal virtues we need to be building into our lives. Few people think of hope as a virtue, but that is what it is. Hope is more than just wishful thinking; it's the deliberate decision to live out of the inevitable conclusion of God's story: the complete redemption of creation. History is going somewhere, and our hope is born again when we fasten it to God's promises and His faithfulness.

In the book of Job a tree is used to underscore human hopelessness in the face of life's hardships. Job was a man who understood the hardships of life. It's not an overstatement to say that at one point he had lost *everything*. In the midst of his darkest times of mourning, confusion, and sorrow, Job lamented the following from the core of his heartache:

> *"We're all adrift in the same boat: too few days, too many troubles. We spring up like wildflowers in the desert and then wilt, transient as the shadow of a cloud. Do you occupy your time with such fragile wisps? Why even bother hauling me into court? There's nothing much to us to start with; how do you expect us to amount to anything? Mortals have a limited life span. You've already decided how long we'll live—you set the boundary and no one can cross it. So why not give us a break? Ease up!*

Even ditchdiggers get occasional days off. For a tree there is always hope. Chop it down and it still has a chance— its roots can put out fresh sprouts. Even if its roots are old and gnarled, its stump long dormant, At the first whiff of water it comes to life, buds and grows like a sapling. But men and women? They die and stay dead. They breathe their last, and that's it. Like lakes and rivers that have dried up, parched reminders of what once was, So mortals lie down and never get up, never wake up again—never." (Job 14:1-14, MSG)

Job thought that it would be better to be a tree than a human, because at least a fallen tree had a chance, however small, of coming back from the trials of this life. Our fate, Job believed, was to eventually get crushed under the weight of life and "never wake up again—never." That's a pretty bleak perspective.

However, we see the symbolism of the tree being used very differently within the first Psalm. Instead of being a symbol of man's lack of hope, the tree is used as a symbol of the profound hope those rooted in a relationship with God can enjoy:

"Blessed is the man who does not walk in the counsel of the wicked or stand in the way of sinners or sit in the seat of mockers. But his delight is in the law of the LORD, and on his law he meditates day and night. He is like a

*tree planted by streams of water, which yields its fruit in
season and whose leaf does not wither. Whatever he does
prospers."* (Psalm 1:1-3)

This hope-filled symbolism also characterizes Jesus' own use of
trees within his teachings. Jesus regularly used the tree as a central image
within his teaching ministry (e.g., Matthew 7:17; Luke 6:44; John 15:1),
and through it highlighted the importance of staying connected to his
love, grace, and power. In John's gospel Jesus repeatedly told his disciples
to stay rooted in him and his teachings:

*"I am the true vine, and my Father is the gardener. He
cuts off every branch in me that bears no fruit, while every
branch that does bear fruit he prunes so that it will be even
more fruitful. You are already clean because of the word
I have spoken to you. Remain in me, and I will remain in
you. No branch can bear fruit by itself; it must remain in
the vine. Neither can you bear fruit unless you remain in
me. I am the vine; you are the branches. If a man remains
in me and I in him, he will bear much fruit; apart from
me you can do nothing."* (John 15:1-4)

"If a man remains in me…he will bear much fruit." I'm positive the
disciples immediately thought of Psalm 1 as Jesus spoke those words,
recognizing their rabbi was echoing the promises found there. What

would have shocked them in particular was the fact that Jesus seemed to be localizing the source of Psalm 1's blessings *in himself!* *He* is the one who causes us to thrive and flourish in our calling to be God's image-bearers in the world—humans fully at home in their relationship to God, each other, themselves, and creation.

In light of this, Job's lament can become a source of transformative encouragement and insight if we read it through a lens that was impossible for him: the lens that we are trees sustained by and rooted in Jesus' life and power:

> *"For a tree there is always hope. Chop it down and it still has a chance— its roots can put out fresh sprouts. Even if its roots are old and gnarled, its stump long dormant, At the first whiff of water it comes to life, buds and grows like a sapling."* (Job 14:7-9, MSG)

Throughout our lives we will face many trials and hardships, but no matter what we face, no matter the forces that plot against us, *in Jesus we will always have an enduring hope.* To live with guaranteed hope is an incredible thing, and that is precisely what is available to us through Jesus.

It doesn't matter what parts of us have been "chopped down" by circumstance, misfortune or the selfish acts of others.

It doesn't matter what places within us feel "old and gnarled" due to bitterness, regret, or shame.

It doesn't matter what aspirations and hopes lie "long dormant" after repeated failure or disillusionment.

In Jesus we can still grow "fresh sprouts" (i.e., new beginnings). We can come back to life, budding and growing like a sapling that's been born again. All Jesus needs is for us to stay rooted in him.

Staying rooted in Jesus

How do you and I stay rooted in Jesus? How do we remain connected to him so that we can experience this great life and extraordinary hope, regardless of the circumstances we find ourselves in? How do we keep Jesus' call to discipleship front and centre, especially when we are assaulted by countless distractions and difficulties? How do we avoid being overwhelmed and choked out by the cares and worries of this life? Staying rooted in Jesus begins with and is sustained by a commitment to four priorities.

Engage the Bible everyday. Whether it means reading, studying, discussing, or memorizing, staying rooted to Jesus means staying rooted to the Scriptures. We need to continually stretch our understanding of what the Bible says and how that should play out in our lives. The gospels should be read consistently and carefully, because declaring ourselves to be a disciple of Jesus means we're trying to embed the values, attitudes, and priorities of Jesus into our lives. The importance of reading, studying, memorizing, and discussing the Bible is a value that most Christians agree on, but few actually practice. However, everyone I see flourishing in their discipleship walk is engaging with the Bible everyday.

Develop a strong prayer life. Developing a strong prayer life is very challenging for most people. Personally, prayer is an area I read about, talk about, and think about more than I actually do anything about. Prayer is very hard for me, because quite honestly it feels like a waste of time. It feels inefficient and sometimes ineffective compared to doing something, but I'm pushing myself beyond those faulty assumptions. I'm in the process of exploring different forms of prayer because I want to develop a strong and intimate relationship with Jesus. This intimacy will never happen if I neglect communicating with him honestly and openly. Although it may not be easy for us, taking time everyday to share our hearts with him, and taking time to listen for his still, small voice is critical to our growth as disciples.

Invest in a local church. I will be the first to say that church can suck. You know it and I know it. But here's the reality: I've never, ever, ever met someone who powerfully inspires me to love and serve Jesus that isn't invested and connected to a local church. I don't think church is some kind of magic bullet when it comes to discipleship. However, I believe that discipleship outside of a church commitment just doesn't work. I also know how tempting it is to bounce around and check out the latest ministry, church, or preacher. But discipleship requires roots, and you can't grow deep roots if you're continually uprooting yourself in order to be a part of the next/new thing. Therefore, if we are serious about discipleship to Jesus we have to make it a priority to plug into and invest in a local church community.

Serve others. Following Jesus as a disciple means we must continually remind ourselves that in Jesus' kingdom the leaders are the ones who serve (Luke 22:26) and greatness is measured by one's ability lay down their life for others (John 15:13). Our days are filled with opportunities to bless and serve others in both simple and profound ways, and Jesus calls us to adopt a servant heart that places our preferences secondary to the interests and needs of those around us. Jesus said that his kingdom is one that will be characterized by servant leadership (Matthew 20:25-28), so if we aren't consistently serving others then we're operating out of ego and self-centredness.

To summarize, engaging the Bible daily, developing a strong prayer life, investing in a local church, and serving others are the four touch points that will enable us to thrive in our discipleship walks through the highs and lows of life. Through these four habits we'll flourish like a tree rooted by streams of water.

These disciplines, however, may strike us as overly simplistic or obvious. Because of this, it's common for us to overlook them in order to look for something that sounds deeper and more profound. But these four practices are the foundations—the root structure—of the Christian faith. If we ignore, dismiss, or abandon them, we'll soon find ourselves feeling very old, gnarled, and lifeless.

After years of discipling, mentoring, and observing many young adults, I've noticed a huge difference between those who just *talked* about these things, and those who actually *did* them. Jesus said a disciple is someone who "hears these words of mine and *puts them into practice*"

(Matthew 7:24, emphasis mine). It's easy to extol the virtues of Bible study and prayer, hold lengthy conversations on the nature of community, and discuss new justice initiatives. However, none of these things lead to transformation in Christ. Those who have been truly transformed are those who have consistently *done* these things and not just *talked* about doing them.

A Tree of Life

In the final chapter of the Bible, the Apostle John records the following:

> *"Then the angel showed me the river of the water of life, as clear as crystal, flowing from the throne of God and of the Lamb down the middle of the great street of the city. On each side of the river stood the tree of life, bearing twelve crops of fruit, yielding its fruit every month. And the leaves of the tree are for the healing of the nations."*
> (Revelation 22:2)

In the new heavens and new earth, God will use trees of life to bring about "the healing of the nations." What that means exactly remains a mystery from our current vantage point, but the good news is we can live in anticipation of that day right now. God wants to take old and gnarled trees (i.e., broken, sinful people) and breathe life into them, giving them an enduring hope that no one can take away. He wants to use these redeemed people—these trees of life—as channels of His power and glory for the healing of the nations.

If you stay rooted in Jesus, God will transform you into a tree of life, bursting with love and hope. He will use your life to offer salvation and healing to a world desperately in need of both. And in the midst of it all, you will be anchored to the enduring hope Paul speaks of in Romans:

> *"For I am convinced that neither death nor life, neither angels nor demons, neither the present nor the future, nor any powers, neither height nor depth, nor anything else in all creation, will be able to separate us from the love of God that is in Christ Jesus our Lord."* (Romans 8:38-39)

Enter the kingdom, grow as a disciple, and flourish under Jesus' empowering leadership. Let his love, grace and power pour out from within you and spread "to the ends of the earth" (Acts 1:8). As you do, prepare to be swept up into something breathtaking and beautiful: the kingdom of God and your unique calling within it.

Continue your journey at
meredisciple.com

Printed in Great Britain
by Amazon.co.uk, Ltd.,
Marston Gate.